# Getting Our Kids
# Back on Track

Janine Bempechat

# Getting Our Kids Back on Track

## Educating Children for the Future

Jossey-Bass Publishers · San Francisco

Jossey-Bass books and products are available through most bookstores. To contact Jossey-Bass directly, call (888) 378-2537, fax to (800) 605-2665, or visit our website at www.josseybass.com.

Substantial discounts on bulk quantities of Jossey-Bass books are available to corporations, professional associations, and other organizations. For details and discount information, contact the special sales department at Jossey-Bass.

TCF Manufactured in the United States of America on Lyons Falls Turin Book. This paper is acid-free and 100 percent totally chlorine-free.

Library of Congress Cataloging-in-Publication Data

Bempechat, Janine, date.
    Getting our kids back on track : educating children for the future / Janine Bempechat.—1st ed.
        p. cm.
    Includes bibliographical references and index.
    ISBN 0-7879-4991-4 (perm. paper)
    1. Education—Parent participation—United States.
2. Home and school—United States. 3. Child rearing—United States. I. Title.
LC225.3 .B45 2000
649'.1—dc21                                        99-050951

FIRST EDITION
HB Printing    10 9 8 7 6 5 4 3 2

*For David, Becca, and Adam,*
*whose love means everything to me*

# Contents

# Preface

For more than twenty years, I have sought to understand the dynamics of high achievement in children ordinarily considered to be at risk for school failure because of family characteristics. Children considered to be at risk may be children of color, or poor, or raised by one parent; they may not speak English at home, or they may have parents who themselves have low levels of education. Over the years, I have seen the varied and creative ways in which many poor and minority parents struggle to provide their children with the best possible education. They are all too familiar with the obstacles their children will face along the educational path to financial security. Whether their children are enrolled in public, parochial, or voucher schools, these are parents who advocate for teachers to expect the most from their children and who want their children to be held to exacting standards for both academic and social behavior. As I discussed in *Against the Odds: How "At Risk" Students Exceed Expectations*, the various factors that put children at risk for school difficulty and failure are not necessarily predictive of dire academic consequences.

The fierce determination of poor parents to ensure that their children are pushed and prodded and prepared for advanced study is nothing less than venerable. At the same time, I am witness to a curious trend in the attitudes of many middle-class parents. In more affluent communities, many parents are expressing increased anger at attempts to infuse their children's schools with the kind of academic rigor for which poor parents clamor. For example, as evidenced by a great many articles in major newspapers and mainstream news magazines, homework has apparently become something of a scourge on daily family life. Many parents argue that teachers and principals need to understand that their children have "a life outside of school," and advocate for a more relaxed academic atmosphere. They are concerned that academic pressure may undermine their children's self-esteem.

These divergent attitudes and approaches to children's education have left me both baffled and concerned. I am baffled because it seems that in some communities, concern about children's self-esteem has taken on a life of its own, having become a tremendous source of anxiety among many parents. I cannot think of another time in our educational history when we have been so consumed with ensuring that our children feel good about themselves. Somehow it does not count that academic competence enhances self-esteem—apparently, academics are not what is important. What really counts is defined outside the academic curriculum: athletics, drama, and the arts. Further, and somewhat ironically, my observations run counter to commonly accepted stereotypes of poor parents as uncaring and uninvolved in their children's schooling, and of middle-class parents as overly involved and anxious that their children be aptly prepared for every educational challenge from preschool forward. So much for stereotypes.

I am concerned because our nation is living through a period of massive underachievement, especially in mathematics and science. Every cross-national assessment of technical achievement seems to bring increasingly depressing news. We have gone from knowing in the early 1980s that Asian students (in Japan, Taiwan, and the People's Republic of China) far surpass their American peers to learning in the late 1990s that the achievement of our students is on par with that of their counterparts in Bosnia, for whom survival is a far more critical issue than cosines and theorem proofs. What is going on?

I believe that the attitudes about schooling of which I speak are indicative of a backlash against the pressures and competitiveness to which many baby-boomer parents were themselves subjected.

Understandably, many parents do not want their children to be pressured as they were, so they are advocating for reduced home-work loads, schoolwork that is not stressful, and increased time and attention for the development of extra-curricular skills. Rather than being seen as opportunities to open minds and increase skills and knowledge, homework and other academic assignments are perceived as intruding on family time, which for many families is at a premium. We are seeing the results in plummeting test scores and, ironically, in parents who are increasingly uneasy about their children's achievement and feeling confused about how to set pri-orities for their children's development without undermining their self-esteem.

I am not merely a passive observer of societal beliefs about edu-cation. I am a parent with two school-age children, and I confront these issues daily. My husband and I have certain ideas about how we want to structure our family life to embrace and foster intellec-tual, social, artistic, and athletic skills. As any parent knows, it is not easy to balance these competing goals, and I find myself mak-ing compromises that do not always make me happy. For example, I would love for my children to come home right after school and do their homework right away. For good or ill, my husband and I have yielded to the culture of "play dates" and after-school lessons in swimming, pottery, and the like. And so, like many parents, we have learned the wisdom of choosing our battles. Clearly, these bat-tles are different in different families. In this book I hope to give you a sense of how you can evaluate for yourself which battles are worth fighting.

It is important for you to know that this book speaks primarily to middle-income parents and their families. Although many issues of schooling and motivation are common to all families, there are issues that are specific to middle-class parents. For example, the dilemmas involved in carpooling children to and from hockey games and soccer practices lie more in the realm of middle-class life, where greater income gives parents the choice of whether and how much to involve their children in extra-curricular activities. In an upcoming work, Norma Jimenez and I will address issues that are pertinent to lower-income families of diverse ethnic and cultural backgrounds.

Undoubtedly our ideas about how to raise our children are influenced by the cultures and contexts in which we ourselves grew up, and I cannot deny my own biases. When I was still an infant, my parents were driven out of Egypt; they immigrated to Montreal, where I grew up. The experience of immigration left an indelible mark on my parents' adaptation to a new and strange society. As it was for families of the Jewish Diaspora, our extended family scattered around the globe and struggled to rebuild their lives. Having no one but themselves to rely on, my parents threw their efforts into our schooling, largely because they perceived that it was the only way to guarantee a secure future. In addition, our culture and religious background places a high value on scholarship. Our home life was thus structured primarily around issues of education.

Having witnessed firsthand the financial struggles my parents endured and the sacrifices they made for the sake of our education, I had, like many children of immigrants, very little difficulty embracing my parents' educational values. However, my own children are one generation removed from the anxiety of the immigrant experience. Will they be as receptive as I was to the necessity of being a good student? Will I push and prod them the way my parents pushed and prodded me? I don't think I can. I did not resent my parents for doing so, but my children might very well resent me. There is no question in my mind but that I will have to adapt my own socialization practices in order to accommodate the very different context in which my children are growing up, and I am not quite sure how to do this. You, then, can expect no easy prescriptions for guaranteeing school success—indeed there are none. Instead, I offer in these pages ways for you to think about the kinds of messages you communicate to your children about schooling and the ways in which you communicate them. The paths to school success are as varied as there are children. My hope is that this book fosters discussions about the different ways we all have to encourage our children to reach their intellectual potential.

My goal is to do this in a caring and supportive way, so I open each chapter with a parent's, child's, or teacher's story, one of many that I have noted over the years in my work with children in Boston's public and Catholic schools. I also include many examples of the trying situations many parents face and the different ways in which they sought to solve their children's academic and motivational difficulties.

## How This Book Is Organized

I open in Chapter One by taking a look at parents' concerns about their children's development, focusing especially on many parents' desire to promote well-roundedness in their children. That children should develop their abilities in many areas (school, athletics, art, and music, for example) is a notion very much shaped by the culture in which we live. Many of us believe that well-rounded children are the ones who are the healthiest from a psychological and social perspective. I argue that well-roundedness, in and of itself, neither guarantees nor predicts well-adjusted children. Instead, I talk about how the desire to foster well-roundedness can undermine your children's progress in school.

In Chapter Two, I look at what educational researchers know about how parents influence the development of their children's beliefs about schooling and learning. We now know, for example, that unreasonably high standards for school achievement can make even the *brightest* children doubt their abilities and become very unsure and anxious about doing well in school. All the objective evidence of their stellar achievements have no influence on their perceptions of their ability. Sadly, their parents' excessively high expectations lead many exemplary students to believe they are not "smart."

I also talk about how problems with motivation, apparent as early as the second grade, are fostered in part by the introduction of formal grading practices, which in turn create greater anxiety in many parents, which in turn are communicated to children in many subtle ways. In this regard, I present common dilemmas faced by parents and make suggestions for how you can resolve them. For example, how should you react to your children's criticism of the teacher?

I open Chapter Three with information on what you can do to support your children's academic achievement. I talk about the different ways that you can promote excitement and dedication to learning, as well as a tolerance for assignments that are neither enjoyable nor fulfilling. I want to make clear, however, that there is no easy or singular formula than can guarantee success for every family or, for that matter, for every child in one family. With this caveat in the open, I take a look at what is generally believed to hold for many families: that structure, predictability, and consistency are helpful for children as they learn to become students.

In particular, I discuss difficulties and dilemmas we all face when our children have to cope with schoolwork they consider to be boring or useless. For example, should you set strict guidelines for how, when, and where homework should be completed? What are the benefits and drawbacks of strict expectations for the fulfillment of assignments? How much help should you provide? How can you know when you are offering too much or too little assistance? Is it inevitable that homework become a task of nightmarish proportions, or are there other ways that you can structure homework to make it an enriching part of daily family life?

My goal in Chapter Four is to show how parents can blend homework into the "quality" time with their children that they so crave. I take a close and critical look at the ongoing and complicated debates about the value of homework. What is the goal of homework? At what point should children have assigned homework? How much should they have at different grade levels? How much is too much? Should parents be involved in their children's homework? If so, what should this involvement look like? Can parents be too involved? And why is the nation engaged in this debate in the first place?

I summarize the educational research that has become well known of late: that homework, especially in elementary school, has no measurable benefit and can indeed undermine children's interest in learning. Despite this well-respected evidence, I argue that this research has neglected to consider the ways in which homework can lay the foundation for a variety of attitudes and approaches to learning that are helpful for school success, including persistence, diligence, and the ability to delay gratification. I then turn to the more pragmatic homework concerns and conflicts with children that parents face on a daily basis.

In Chapter Five I talk about how you can work to support your teachers' values as well as your own educational priorities. Undoubtedly I touch on concerns that are very sensitive, but they need to be articulated. Supporting the work of the teacher requires you to balance reasoned judgments with your own perceptions and interpretations of your teacher's behavior toward your children. There are times when doing so is neither easy nor straightforward. Does this imply that you should show unqualified support for your children's teacher? As much as is possible, yes. Nonetheless, I believe that it is entirely appropriate and necessary for you to advocate for your children—to question your teacher's attitudes and behaviors toward your children—if you believe they are being treated unfairly.

My purpose in Chapter Six is to debate the enduring problems that many parents face as their children's interests become more varied and their attentions are increasingly divided between schoolwork and extra-curricular activities. Most parents are delighted to encourage interest and involvement in activities outside of school. What can you do, though, when you are confronted with falling grades in school? Should you consider extra-curricular activities to be a privilege that can be withdrawn in the face of dropping grades? What if you believe that your children's self-esteem is inexorably linked to a particular outside interest? Is it appropriate to pull children out of an activity they value, or does this strategy have the potential to do more harm than good? And why has this issue of balance reached such a stress-producing level for many families?

In Chapter Seven I look at the phenomenon that educational researchers have come to call the *antiachievement ethic*, which emerges, not surprisingly, around the transition into adolescence. This is a time when youngsters are trying to develop a sense of personal identity separate from their parents. Many students become contrary, difficult, or rebellious around issues both social and academic. It is also a time when many teenagers want desperately to fit in. Child psychologists consider this defiance to be "developmentally appropriate"—in other words, a natural part of growing up.

It is not clear to me, as a parent, how much "developmentally appropriate" behavior is appropriate. And so I ask, What happens among peers when it becomes "uncool" to do well in school? How do seemingly well-adjusted students come to endorse this position? What can you do to navigate your children away from this view? What can you do to help your children cope with the difficulties that arise when they are belittled by their peers for being "too" smart or "too" hard working? What can you do or say to counter peers' encouragement to "tone down" their success in school? Are there ways for you to lay the groundwork early to provide a kind of inoculation against negative peer pressure? In other words, what kinds of attitudes and beliefs about learning can you convey early in your children's lives that might help them develop resilience against these kinds of oppositional messages?

I close the book in Chapter Eight by arguing that all parents need to keep in mind a larger vision for their children as they strive to prepare them for the significant challenges that lie ahead. I believe that ultimately we must be vigilant about the tremendous influence we have in shaping and remolding our children's attitude toward schooling—vigilant about what we communicate about our children's schools and their teachers, vigilant to our children's developing beliefs about learning and its relation to their future, vigilant about how our children are interpreting their day-to-day experiences with teachers and peers alike, and vigilant about how we set priorities for our children's development. We all have within us the ability to help our children reach their intellectual potential. We can do this if we remain focused on the larger vision we have for our children's futures.

## Acknowledgments

I extend great appreciation to my many students, who over the years have generously shared with each other and with me their beliefs and convictions about children's schooling and educational reform. To all those in my Achievement Motivation courses and seminars who worked with me, argued with me, yelled at me, and otherwise implored me to see schooling from their diverse points of view, I thank you for your contributions to the discussions and debates that became part and parcel of our attempts to understand how parents contribute to their children's success in school.

I am deeply indebted to my friend and colleague Norma Jimenez, who gave up precious time to read multiple drafts of this manuscript and lend her considerable knowledge and insights to the ideas I present in this book. In particular, I wish to acknowledge Norma's feedback and contributions to the revisions of the final draft. Norma is one of the best teachers I have ever had, and my work is strengthened by her wisdom.

I am grateful to have benefited from the help and advice given to me by Beth Delamater, a soon-to-be graduate of our doctoral program. Beth wrote the Helpful Questions section, and this book is the better for her insights.

I am blessed to have worked again with Leslie Berriman at Jossey-Bass. Leslie has the uncanny ability to turn a casual conversation into a book, and this is the second time she has done this for me. Her thoughtful comments and criticisms are always on the mark, and she never fails to deliver them with good humor. Leslie is truly a master of motivation.

Once again, I am grateful to the faculty at the Mason-Rice School in Newton Centre, who lent me their professional knowledge and experience through their careful reading of earlier drafts. Mark Springer, principal, and first- and second-grade teachers Tom Daniels and Anne Marie Osiecki provided invaluable perspectives on the views I express in this book. During the course of my writing, I have received tremendous support from my friends Leslie Anderson, Amy Cooper, Joan Hutchinson, Susan Simon, and Laurie Striar. All graciously agreed to read initial drafts and share with me the wisdom of their experiences with their own children. My writing is strengthened for their advice.

At the Harvard Graduate School of Education, I continue to be blessed with the gift of high expectations from my teachers and mentors: Catherine Snow, Bob LeVine, Howard Gardner, and Bob Selman. My friends and colleagues Susan Holloway, Mike Nakkula, Cathy Ayoub, and Suzanne Graham tolerate my rants over coffee, the rare lunch, and e-mail. Each comes to the question of parental influences in children's learning from different theoretical and research perspectives. They challenge my ideas, and I am the grateful recipient of their good sense and understanding.

Once more, I thank Star Herman, Brett Kosineski, and Lisa Gillin of Seattle's Best Coffee, in Newton Centre, where I wrote this book in the gracious company of young women and men who kept me going with great coffee and smiles of encouragement.

I would not have been able to devote myself to my writing as I have were it not for the love and support that Tracey Doherty gives our family every day. Her devotion sustains us all. Finally, my deepest thanks and appreciation go to my husband, David, and my children, Becca and Adam, who patiently endured another stretch of time when I was "at the café." They are my light and my love.

# Getting Our Kids Back on Track

# CHAPTER 1

# Challenging Our Assumptions

> My children spend five hours in school every day.
> They work very hard while they are there, and
> believe me, it's stressful. The last thing they need is
> homework. They need to come home and relax.
> They have to have a life outside of school.
> —*Mother of fourth-grade twins*

As an educational researcher and parent of two school-age children, I find this mother's perspective troubling. Regrettably, we find ourselves entering the millennium with our children's competence in mathematics, science, and technology increasingly at risk. Our youngsters' proficiency in mathematics and science sits at alarmingly low levels relative to that of their peers in most other industrialized nations. What's more, this is old news. We have known since the early 1980s that North American primary and secondary school students lag well behind their Japanese, Taiwanese, and Chinese counterparts in math and science achievement. More recently, large-scale studies of over forty industrialized nations have added fuel to the underachievement fire. We now know that, relative to their peers in France, Germany, England, and many other nations, our students consistently rank in the bottom fourth in all disciplines of mathematics, including algebra, geometry, functions, and probability. This is simply not a good time to let down our collective educational guard.

You may ask, Why should we be so worried? After all, as the wealthiest nation, the United States enjoys the highest standard of living in the world. Do not be lulled into a false sense of security. The reality is that when our children come of age to contribute to this wealth, all indications are that they will be ill prepared. Economic survival, at an individual and societal level, depends on technologically relevant skills, and we have been and continue to be coming up short, so to speak.

Where academic achievement is concerned, we are a second-rate nation, and we need to get back on track. This book is a call to action for parents. We need to help our children and our nation get through this educational crisis. I believe that the "school reform movement," which means different things to different players, has failed to address the one issue that is in need of urgent attention—our wanting attitudes about academic achievement. We need a radical shift, not only in curricula, teacher training, and public school management but also in our attitudes about schooling and learning. If we are serious about improving academic achievement, we need to resolve our ambivalence about academic excellence. In particular,

- We need to worry less about self-esteem and more about competence.
- We need to expect much more from our children.
- We need to challenge our children to confront difficulty.
- We need to teach our children that disciplined effort makes all the difference in learning.
- We need to take our children's education much more earnestly.
- We need to rein in our commitment to extra-curricular activities.

I know that much of what I say goes against the grain of what many educators and psychologists believe about healthy psychological and social development. And I know that what I believe may sound shocking and mean spirited, but hear me out. I too am a parent of school-age children, and I want nothing more than for them to be happy and to feel good about themselves. Yet I believe that we are far too concerned with our children's happiness and self-esteem, to the detriment of their ability to cope with difficulty and setbacks. From my perspective in this debate, self-esteem is overrated, and the collective hysteria over whether children have enough of it has taken on a life of its own, one that was never anticipated by educational researchers study its development. Why is this?

The demographic, societal, and economic changes that took place from the 1960s through the 1990s led to great increases in the percentage of children who are at risk for school failure and other problem behaviors, such as drug and alcohol abuse and precocious sexuality. Poverty, single parenthood, parents with low levels of education, and limited English proficiency are factors that have contributed, either singly or in combination, to childhood psychological and social difficulties of epidemic proportions. A great many youngsters are living with and through issues that are far beyond their years, such as teen pregnancy and parenthood.

The response of many psychologists, educators, and community workers has been to place children's salvation in increasing their self-esteem. The thinking, apparently, is that if we can get kids to feel better about themselves, we can chip away at the problems that threaten their development into healthy and productive citizens. Increasing self-esteem has become the benchmark of intervention programs, and virtually everyone who works with children, whether or not those children live troubled lives, works to ensure that they have high self-esteem.

The problem is that, in the service of this illusive goal, we have embraced assumptions that are undermining our very efforts to help children *genuinely* feel better about themselves. For example, doing poorly in school understandably threatens self-esteem; being held back in school has a negative influence on self-esteem. However, rather than throwing our considerable knowledge behind programs that provide remediation (a dirty word in some education circles), we have instead embraced lower standards and "social promotion," a truly failed policy that has led to students who are functionally illiterate being graduated from high school.

Our intent is good, but that does not excuse us from letting down generations of children. High self-esteem is not a gift that we can wrap and offer up as a birthday present. When we make it easy to attain goals that would otherwise be difficult for anyone to attain, we are doing a terrible disservice to the children who most need our help.

I know from my personal experiences and my work with children in classrooms that we cannot and *should not* orchestrate our children's experiences to ensure happiness. Many parents seem desperate to protect their children from challenges, setbacks, and failure. They fear that these unpleasant experiences and the resulting feelings of sadness, frustration, and anger might undermine their children's self-esteem. In the long run, it is *precisely* these unpleasantries that allow for the greatest growth and maturity.

We do no one, least of all our children, any favors when we try to shield them from difficulty. It is in the face of difficulty and challenge that children learn to cope with the kinds of obstacles that everyone eventually encounters. If children only experience success that comes easily, they are certain to fall apart at the first sign of failure. The first failure may come in the fourth grade, when they begin reading for understanding rather than reading for content. Or it may come in the transition to middle school, when they lose the closeness of learning from one teacher in the company of the same peers. Or it may come in high school, when schools become much larger and increasingly impersonal.

The first failure may even come in college or graduate school or the first job—in this sense it doesn't matter when. What matters is that it *will* happen, despite our efforts as loving and caring parents to prevent it. We will have unwittingly sent our children out into the world unprepared to bounce back from trying experiences. In other words, we will have robbed them of critical early opportunities to develop strategies that will foster resilience in the face of failure.

I am not proposing that we let our children wallow in quicksand. I am suggesting that we view discouraging experiences, theirs as well as our own, as opportunities to demonstrate how to cope with disappointment—as teachable moments, if you will. Goodness knows, none of us has to stage unpleasant experiences; they occur in daily life. We get lost driving to a new place. We rearrange our schedule to wait at home for the service person who never shows up. We stay up very late to prepare for a meeting that is canceled at the last minute. We find out that we unwittingly offended a good friend. How we react to daily challenges speaks volumes to our children about how to deal with ourselves and others when things do not go our way.

In order to give our children the opportunities to experience and cope with challenges, we need to raise our expectations and standards for their academic achievement. Barring the assignment of projects that are inappropriate for their age, children are capable of doing much, much more than we give them credit for. Complaining to teachers that assignments are too hard and take too long to do serves no purpose other than to undermine the teacher's efforts to teach and our children's efforts to learn. Children learn nothing from easy assignments. That they don't does not bother me nearly as much as what they may come to *believe* as a result of easy assignments. For example, some students can come to believe that school is a breeze, that they are really smart. Worse still, others can come to believe that the only reason the teacher gives them easy work is because he or she feels they are "stupid" and could not possibly complete more involved assignments.

Both beliefs are dangerous. In the first case, children are lulled into a false sense of intellectual security. Eventually they will encounter schoolwork that will be hard to do, and they will have no choice but to believe they are not smart enough to master it. Their balloon of high confidence is bound to burst, with very trying consequences. Previously unencountered struggles may very well leave them baffled, demoralized, and at a loss for what to do next. In the second case, the consequences for learning are disastrous: children are drawn into believing that they lack the ability to master more interesting and challenging schoolwork. If they believe they are "dumb," then there is no point in investing effort in learning. This is indeed a very high price for students to pay for *our* desire that they not be challenged or stressed in school. They cannot possibly acquire the skills they need, at the level at which they need them, unless we give them homework and other assignments that push them to reason, analyze, and synthesize information in new and creative ways.

## The Need for Homework

And so, beginning with kindergarten, all children need to have appropriately challenging homework to do after school. Homework is critical because it is the training ground for the development of qualities that we all want so much to see in our children: responsibility, diligence, persistence, and the ability to delay gratification. Children need time, and lots of it, in which to nurture these personal qualities. With very few exceptions, we cannot possibly expect students to develop these strengths of character overnight. It is the nature of childhood that youngsters are egocentric and demanding. None of us would expect a two-year-old to share her toys willingly and to wait patiently for her turn at the swings. Yet we do expect this kind of behavior from a five-year-old about to enter kindergarten. This transformation in children's behavior between two and five years of age does not happen magically. All of us can attest to the energy and time it takes over thousands of experiences, big and small, to mold the impatient and unreasonable two-year-old into the relatively composed five-year-old. And so it is with the "habits of mind" of which I speak. We cannot possibly expect children entering middle school to be efficient learners if they have had minimal exposure to homework throughout elementary school. They too need those thousands of experiences, big and small, to develop the endurance, persistence, and willingness to tolerate uncertainty that are expected of them by the time they enter the sixth grade. These skills do not emerge spontaneously—they evolve over time and as a result of a lot of effort on the part of parents and their children.

## The Need for Disciplined Effort

For many children, effort is akin to a double-edged sword. On the one hand, they know that they need to try in order to do well, but on the other hand, if they *have* to try, it means they are not smart. Rather than being a tool that can enhance their abilities, effort becomes a pure and simple condemnation of their abilities. We need to get children to see that *disciplined* effort can indeed enhance their abilities and make them "smarter." It is through struggle that students deepen their understanding of material, and an ever-deepening understanding gives them the insights that lead to higher-order thinking skills, including the ability to evaluate and think critically.

Children's beliefs about how smart they are do not take firm hold until the fourth or fifth grade. The early elementary school years (kindergarten through second grade), then, are the prime years in which we can teach children strategies for coping with difficulty and confusion. We need to capitalize on these years to present children with learning experiences that foster resilience in the midst of difficulty and setbacks. Doing so will not guarantee that a child will become a highly confident student, but it will give many children a leg up on learning how to confront disappointment and failure.

## The Need to Value Scholarship

Despite the political rhetoric, we are a nation that does not value academic excellence. Our winning quarterbacks get far more accolades than do our exemplary student writers and mathematicians. In fact, missing a practice session or, heaven forbid, a game is a grave offense that carries with it punitive consequences of a most serious nature, including being benched for a few games. Yet somehow it has become increasingly acceptable to many parents that their children miss school, not for illness but to take or lengthen a family vacation. In addition, many parents see no problem in acknowledging that everyone needs to take a "mental health" day every now and again—a day to sit back, cool off, and refresh oneself. Thus some children miss a day of school here and there over the course of an academic year.

I would love to take a mental health day myself. Goodness knows, writing this book has taken a lot out of me. A few days off would have done me a world of good. But I have not taken a day off, not because I am an exemplary person but because I have an obligation to my editor, who has an obligation to the people in her publishing group and company. If I am late, everyone else is late.

Certainly no real harm or long-lasting intellectual damage will arise from children's missing a few days of school here and there. However, inasmuch as I have an obligation to my editor, my children have obligations to their teachers, and my husband and I feel strongly that they need to know this. For example, one day in mid-February, waking up to a cold and cloudy Boston day, my seven-year-old daughter announced that she was not going to school because she was tired. "Tough," I said. "Why should you have the day off when everyone else has to be there? And what about Mrs. Jones? Maybe she doesn't feel like teaching you today, but she will because she has to—it's her job. I bet a bunch of kids also don't feel like going to school today, but they'll all be there, along with you." And off she went, mumbling something about grown-ups and unfairness.

Our children can't have it both ways, and neither can we. We simply cannot espouse the singular importance of education to our children while noting times at which it turns out not to be so important. I have no doubt that such inconsistency leaves many children confused about how committed their parents really are to their schooling.

## The Need to Balance

In this context, I am convinced that youngsters today are involved in far too many activities outside of school. Gone are the days when children came home, did their homework, and played in the street until dinnertime. This is largely a sign of the times. Sadly, we no longer live in a society where we can happily send our children out to play with the caveat that they be home by 6:00 P.M. Concerns for our children's safety have given rise to an incredible increase in scheduled activities, many of which occur on school nights. Factor in part-time jobs for our teenagers, and you can see how a given day can be broken up into too many events that compete with schoolwork.

Why are we allowing this? For right or wrong, we live in a society that values well-roundedness. We want our children to develop their talents across a range of skills and abilities, to be good students, to have friends, to be involved in sports and music, and to express their artistic creativity. We believe that helping our children develop their skills in all these areas will enhance their self-esteem; we believe this so strongly that we view children who are "only good in school" as problematic, and describe them disparagingly as nerds, geeks, and brainiacs.

For many parents, involvement in extra-curricular activities is sometimes more about their own self-esteem than their child's. And so, when confronted with worsening grades in school, many parents are loathe to do what comes naturally to others: pull their children out of extra-curricular activities. Increasingly, I see parents viewing involvement in outside activities not as privileges but as essential elements for enhancing self-esteem and maintaining the commitment they need to demonstrate on college applications. And, surprisingly, some parents are finding support among their children's teachers and school counselors.

For example, my colleague Nancy found herself completely undermined by her twelve-year-old daughter's social studies teacher, Mr. Jackson. Her daughter Janie went from a B to a C in this course, and Nancy reiterated the family's rule that forbids participation in extra-curricular activities when report cards grades are lower than a B. Nancy explained that she would not allow Janie to play spring softball so that she would have more time to devote to her studies. Her daughter, bitterly disappointed, mentioned this in passing to Mr. Jackson, who openly disagreed with her mother. He believed very strongly that students should participate in sports. "School isn't everything," he said. To help Janie out, he awarded her an undeserved B so that she could get around her family's rule and play softball.

I have no doubt that Mr. Jackson believed he was acting in Janie's best interests. Unfortunately, his "benevolence" in the service of her self-esteem did her much more harm than good. His actions trivialized her family's standards for her school performance. More seriously, he held Janie to a much lower standard than he did the other students, an act that is patently unfair to her and everyone else. Her B is not the same as everyone else's B; in other words, she knows that her teacher was willing to accept substandard work from her but not from others. Is that because he thought she could not do the work? Janie will never really know. But her high school transcript will show that she was a member of the varsity softball team for four years.

## The Need to Address College Admissions Standards

Our concerns over well-roundedness have not evolved in a vacuum. College admissions and financial aid policies have been complicit in the collective hysteria over well-roundedness. It is not enough anymore to be an exemplary student and to serve the community admirably. Any hope of our children getting into the best colleges rests on their demonstrating their competence in a variety of domains. So the pressure is on to be a top student, a record-holding athlete, a competition-winning musician, and an integral member of the community's soup kitchen.

Prestigious admissions and scholarships are going to our "well-rounded" students, which of course puts the pressure on us as parents to make sure our children are not left in the dust. We scurry around to give them opportunities that we think will look good on their application. We rise at 4:00 A.M. to get to the rink for her hour of practice time, drive him and half a dozen of his buddies to two soccer practices and one game each week, drop her off at her part-time job, get him to the nursing home for his three-hour shift as a volunteer, and so on, and so on. In their zeal to attract well-rounded students, many colleges, especially the top-tier schools, unwittingly shut out many exemplary students. I cannot pretend to know how we can work our way out of this cycle. I believe that institutions of higher learning need to revisit and refine their beliefs about the kind of college applicant best suited to make important contributions to society and to the communities in which they will live, work, and raise their children.

Some colleges may have begun to adopt a more reasonable admission policy by targeting or "angling" their search for students. In other words, at some schools, recruitment officers are asked to identify exemplary prospective students who can fill a particular need, whether in the orchestra, student newspaper, or one or more of the college's athletic teams. To the extent that a shift in college admissions practices may be under way, it is a change that does not necessarily stem from concerns over students' well-being, but rather from a desire to maintain a school's standing in a particular area for which it is known.

## The Need to Rethink Schooling

I know of very few educators who would advocate a "back to basics" approach that would maximize the development of the *academic* child and minimize the development of the *whole* child, and that is not the approach I am advocating. The proverbial pendulum cannot be allowed to swing back *that* far. Yet, given the current state of educational underachievement in our nation, we need to rethink the ways in which we factor schooling into our children's daily lives. We need to swing the pendulum back to some reasonable middle ground, one that acknowledges that children need opportunities to grow and express themselves in a variety of ways and in a context that places academic achievement firmly at the top of every family's list of priorities. This is a tall order, and in the chapters that follow I will share with you my views and recommendations for concrete steps you can take now to enhance your children's academic success. I have no doubt that we can turn things around and get our children, and our nation, back on track.

# CHAPTER 2

# Talking to Your Children About School

*Ali (tenth grader):* I *hate* geometry! I'm never going to
use it in my life. It's the *stupidest* thing in the
world, and I can't see one good reason why I
need to take it.

*Amy (her mom):* It trains your mind to think logically.

*Ali (eyes rolling):* Yeah, right . . .

*Amy:* OK, here's the deal. You need it to get into college. I don't care if you don't like it. There are lots
of things you're going to have to do that you
don't want to do to end up where you want to
be. Get over it.

When you take the time to think about the kinds of things you say
to your children about schooling and education, you realize that
much of your efforts are centered on giving them encouragement.
In all likelihood, encouraging our children is the primary way in
which all of us try to motivate them to work hard to do as well as
they can in school. Many of you may find Amy's comments to be
somewhat caustic, and she does not appear, at first blush, to be the
picture of parental encouragement. Indeed, I cannot really make
the case that Amy is being sympathetic to her daughter's distress.
But this is *precisely* what I like the most about Amy: she knows

when to put her arm around Ali to comfort her and when to tell her to give it up altogether. Ali doesn't know it, but in Amy's inability to be moved by Ali's plight, Amy is giving her daughter a great gift: the realization that things will sometimes, but not always, go her way in life. When you multiply this example by the hundreds of times Amy has probably said things like this, what you end up with in Ali is a young woman who will be able to tolerate difficulty and challenges.

The things we say about learning, as innocuous as they may seem to us, profoundly influence children's beliefs about their abilities. These beliefs, for the large part, dictate the extent to which children embrace or shy away from challenge, and the degree to which they will persist or fall apart in the face of difficulty or confusion.

## Talking About Mistakes

Mistakes Are Our Friends

—*Banner inside the doorway*
*of an elementary school*

When our children are three to five years of age, we are all justifiably thrilled to watch them as their scribbles become recognizable letters and their pretend reading gives way to the understanding that every letter is associated with a specific sound. Throughout these day-care or preschool years, we are relatively calm and content as we witness our children's intellectual development. We expect that children will progress at relatively different rates, and most of us understand that this is just the way it is supposed to be. Unless alerted by the teacher of some emerging learning difficulty, many of us take our children's slower development in stride. After all, whatever differences we see between children at this point in their development tend to even out eventually.

But with the onset of elementary school, many of us go from taking casual and delightful pride in our children's accomplish-

ments to being consumed with class rank. Although we are by
no means inattentive to our children's development during the
preschool years, there is something about the beginning of formal
schooling that makes us that much more vigilant about our children's progress. That "something" is the introduction of conven-
tional evaluations. In other words, we are for the first time on the
receiving end of grades and report cards that let us know just how
well our children are doing. To the extent that we share this information with other parents (as many of us do), we now are also privy
to how our children are progressing relative to others.

Our reactions to the reality of the educational system speak
volumes to our children about the things that we think are the
most important about learning. In very subtle but powerful ways,
we let our children know how much importance we place on "getting everything right"—in other words, minimizing mistakes. Take,
for example, the thinking that Frank, father of a third grader, has
done about his daughter's spelling:

> It's the craziest thing. Debbie studies and practices her
> spelling words every week, and gets all her words right
> on each spelling test. But then when we get her writ-
> ten work back from the teacher, it is riddled with
> what seem, to me at least, to be the most careless mis-
> takes possible. And volumes of them! They appear in
> stories that are ten, twenty pages long, mini chapter
> books, you name it. We love to have her read them to
> us—they're hilarious! My wife keels over half the
> time! I have to tell you—at this point, I prefer that
> she write and enjoy writing, which she clearly does,
> than have perfect spelling.

Plainly, Frank is not *un*concerned about Debbie's tendency to
make many spelling mistakes when she writes, but neither is he *so*
consumed that he reacts like Nadia, a mother in the class who is
having a somewhat similar problem with her son:

This is completely ridiculous and, frankly, unacceptable. The reality is that it looks really bad to be making these kinds of spelling mistakes at his age. No one but Jack gets words like *right* and *goal* wrong. What's the teacher going to think, for heaven's sake? So I told him that we are going to practice the week's words every night, and when he has to write his story in class on Fridays, I told him to use *only* the words we have practiced and *only* if he is sure he remembers how to spell them.

Confronted with the same problem, these two parents are communicating very different messages to their children. Debbie knows that her parents most value the creative and funny stories she writes; she hardly realizes that she makes more mistakes than other kids in the class. The fact that Frank and his wife revel in Debbie's stories only reinforces their emphasis on the *process* of learning how to write: how to compose a story that has rich details and a clear beginning, middle, and end. In contrast, Jack knows that his mother places a premium on correct spelling and is very concerned about what the teacher will think about *her* if he keeps making mistakes. When he brings his stories home, she checks first for errors and then pays attention to the content. Nadia does not say much about what Jack writes about, and at this point he doesn't much care either. Not surprisingly, he focuses all his attention on making sure he does not make spelling mistakes. And he is acutely aware of where his spelling ability stands in relation to the other children in his classroom. In no way am I suggesting that Frank is a better parent than Nadia. I am stating, though, that Frank is doing a better job of fostering a love of writing in his child. As parents, we can do little about competition in the classroom, but we *can* exercise control over our reactions to our children's mistakes.

It is not easy to watch young children make mistakes, and say nothing. The reality of how painful it can be to watch children struggle was made clear to me by my daughter's first-grade teacher, who was delighted to have me volunteer once a week at writing time but was dismayed that I felt compelled to tell the children how to spell certain words when they asked for my help. I, in turn, was mortified to witness what has come to be known as "invented" spelling: the spelling of words exactly as you hear them pronounced. What I saw was a mumbo-jumbo of "words" that were strung to-gether as if on a clothesline, with no separation anywhere. The "words," if you can call them that, had no vowels, only consonants. What was the sense in this? After all, wasn't this the best time in the children's schooling to teach them how to spell—to "strike while the iron was hot," so to speak?

With the teacher's coaching, I learned that the consequences of my approach would have been the following: with their at-tention turned to the "right" way to spell, they would have begun writing much less, been very conscious of mistakes, and begun en-tertaining notions that they were not "good" writers, all of which would have spelled disaster for their intrinsic love of writing. In other words, my desire to control their writing would have inhib-ited them from writing. I do not wish to leave you with the impres-sion that these children never learned to spell. Indeed they did, but the focus on spelling, grammar, and sentence construction began a year later, when the children had developed their own identities as writers. When your children begin to study spelling, it is terribly important to use their mistakes as *learning tools*. In other words, call attention to your children's mistakes, not as a means to show your disappointment in their performance but as a way to help them un-derstand the cause of their mistakes and develop strategies for working their way through similarly difficult problems.

Despite how smart some children are (or think they are), they will eventually come up against material they do not understand at first glance. They will have to endure confusion and frustration. The short stories (or long ones, as in Debbie's case) of first grade will give way to increasingly complex writing assignments. For example, in the fifth grade, Debbie and her classmates will be required to do library research, say, on the lives of African Americans before and after abolition. They will have to summarize material from multiple sources, write detailed descriptions of historical accounts, offer comparisons and contrasts between both time periods, and provide their own analyses of the extent to which life may or may not have changed after abolition.

Debbie will be equal to the task. By virtue of having been encouraged to write from first grade forward, with little *initial* regard for her spelling mistakes, she will evolve into the writer her fifth-grade teacher expects her to be. She will certainly face moments of confusion—wondering if she has gathered too much or too little material, for example. Her accumulated writing experience will leave her better equipped emotionally to cope with the frustrations that come from completing such a demanding assignment. I doubt that she will do so happily. It is terribly unpleasant to feel lost, but Debbie will at least be equipped with a variety of strategies, accumulated over time, that will help her cope with confusion. In other words, her parents' openness to academic challenge and mistakes gives Debbie the gift of resilience and confidence. In contrast, by trying to orchestrate academic success, Nadia is unwittingly setting Jack up for failure, disappointment, and a relative inability to cope with either.

- Let your children know that they are bound to fail if they avoid mistakes.
- Praise the *process* your child has gone through to produce her "chapter book," math story, or report on life in medieval times.
- Judge your child's performance by the progress he has made since the last evaluation, not by how well or poorly he compares to others.
- Encourage your child to opt for challenging assignments over easy ones.
- Think about *how*, not *whether*, your child can successfully complete an assignment.

## Talking About Intelligence

I'm not good at math, I have never been good at
math, and I will *never* be good at math. That's it.

—*Eddy, tenth grader*

I know that even if I have to break my head open,
I can do well in calculus.

—*Gisell, tenth grader*

We live in a society that has its own peculiar view about what intelligence is and what people who are intelligent look like. Most of us believe that intelligence is innate—that some of us are born smarter than others. In other words, we believe that our children come into the world with a certain amount of intelligence and that this "allotment" is pretty much what they will have to work with the rest of their lives. We unquestioningly believe that smart children learn quickly and effortlessly and are incredibly lucky—everything is going to go their way in life. (In fact, it will not necessarily be so, as we will discuss later on.)

The rest of our children have to make do with what their genes have seen fit to endow them. Because they're not as smart as "So-and-So," they are going to have to try harder than him or her in order to do well in school. Even then, despite their efforts, there's a limit to how much they are going to be able to learn. Let's face it: how many of them are destined to be the next Madeleine Albright, I. M. Pei, Mimi Leder, Michael Eisner, Susan Love, or Robert Gallo?

This view of intelligence as *limited* and *limiting* influences how we talk to our children about their learning experiences, both good and bad. This is how Dina is talking to her teenager, Eddy, about his failing grade in algebra:

I really want you to do better in Algebra I—you'll
need it for college—but here's the thing—and I'll be
honest with you. I was never good at math either. It

was always a terrible struggle for me. You just have to try hard and do the best you can.

Dina is communicating an important message that she hopes will boost her son's morale and motivation. She is clear in her expectation that he should do better in math. Yet she is being completely candid in sharing with Eddy the fact that she too struggled a great deal with math. In so doing, she is conveying her empathy and demonstrating that she herself really knows what Eddy is going through. Dina's compassionate understanding lets Eddy know that she is not angry with the grades he is bringing home. Quite to the contrary, she is being appreciative of his difficulties and accepting of his performance, at least for now.

This attentive and involved mother would be horrified to know that her efforts to support her son through a stressful academic experience are likely to have an effect the exact opposite of what she intended. To be sure, Dina is being very understanding of the problems Eddy is having with algebra. It is not easy to feel completely confused and, worse still, to know that most everyone else understands what is going on. Unfortunately, by saying that she herself was never "good" at math, Dina with her well-intentioned remarks is communicating her belief that success in mathematics depends very much on innate ability, of which she believes she was meagerly endowed. It is not a far stretch, then, for Eddy to believe that he too may lack the necessary ability to succeed in math.

The danger lies not so much with this particular belief as with its consequences for learning and motivation. When students believe that they lack what they perceive to be the necessary ability to master a skill, in their minds it makes no sense to try, so Dina's entreaties to "put his best foot forward" are likely to fall on deaf ears. The actual setting matters little; it could be the classroom, the basketball court, or the piano lesson. The end result is the same: students who believe they are "dumb" are left with nowhere to go, as it were. There is simply nothing that can compensate for lack of ability. Or is there?

What if Dina viewed intelligence the way Sheila, Gisell's mother, does? Instead of seeing it as something that is *limited* and *limiting*, Sheila thinks of intelligence as something that can be enhanced through effort. Her comments show that she believes effort can *activate* intelligence—bring it to life, so to speak:

> Look, I was never a math whiz, but here's the thing. By the time I was in fourth grade, I realized that I was not as smart in math as some of my friends. So I decided, fine, I'm not as smart as Wendy, but I *can* do as well as she can. I just have to work a heck of a lot harder to get the good grades she does. Mark my words, wherever you go in life, you'll find people who are stronger than you and people who are weaker than you. You just have to focus on yourself and what *you* can do to get where you want to be.

Intelligence, in and of itself, is not an inoculation against the kinds of beliefs about learning that can undermine children's academic progress; many "smarter" children often suffer the greatest difficulties with motivation. All of us know children who fit the description of the classic underachiever: very intelligent but not fulfilling their potential. They tend to stick to what they know how to do, are very conscious of avoiding mistakes and looking "dumb," and fall apart or shut down at the first sign of difficulty. Their intelligence, however high it may be, is not helping them overcome this hurdle.

However, we also know children who are not that "smart" but who attain levels of proficiency we may never have predicted from their IQ scores. They are the first ones to jump in to volunteer for a new and different project, one that offers no guarantee of success.

They seem to be undaunted by failure or setbacks, and they get right back on their proverbial horses when they fall off. It would never occur to them to see mistakes as implicit condemnations of their intelligence; mistakes are simply part and parcel of "getting the hang of it." These children are helped along not by their "intelligence" as much as their determination to learn and persist and their willingness to make mistakes and learn from failure. In other words, they have the *motivational* qualities that will see them through difficult learning experiences. In the long run, these students may very well end up "smarter" than their "smart" peers. That is to say, by virtue of having avoided academic challenge, some of the students we all consider to be so intelligent will have unwittingly deprived themselves of opportunities to learn new things and increase their skills and knowledge.

Personally, I have never thought of myself as a *really* smart person. I do not think I am very "intelligent." Many of you reading this book might be thinking what I would be thinking if I were in your shoes: that I am being modest or self-effacing. After all, I *am* a Harvard professor (an assistant professor, but a professor nonetheless). Some subjects came relatively easily to me in school, especially the language arts. But as I like to tell my students, I suffered more than anyone I know and shed rivers of tears to get through the sequence of mathematics courses I had to take in order to get into college and then graduate school. Yet you would never know it to see my transcripts, peppered as they are with A's in virtually every algebra, calculus, and statistics course I ever took. It was not always this way. I recall doing fine until about the fourth grade, when suddenly nothing in math seemed to make sense to me anymore. I remember telling my father that no one asked any questions in class and that I was afraid to, because then everyone would know that I was dumb. He said, "Ask all you want, and know that three-quarters of the class will be happy you did, because *they* don't know what's going on either."

It was such a small thing that he said, yet it had a profound influence on how I dealt with math from that point forward. I just knew in my heart that if I was going to do well, I would have to work harder than probably everyone else in the world, and be the one who asked all the "dumb" questions. And now that I have children of my own, I do not wish for them to be *really* smart. I want them to know that they can do whatever it is they wish to do in life, provided they keep plugging away, as aggravating and frustrating as that may be.

After twenty years of studying children's beliefs about intelligence, I have finally come to my own understanding. There are people who are much smarter than I am, and I will never be able to match their level of understanding, no matter how hard I try. *But,* and this is a big But, I believe very strongly that I can master anything I need to master in order to move my education and my career forward. Twenty years ago, I would never have imagined having the opportunity to learn from and now work alongside so many truly intelligent scholars who have contributed so much to our understanding of child development and personality: Howard Gardner, Catherine Snow, Robert LeVine, Jerome Kagan, and David McClelland, to name but a few.

Most children do not necessarily have the natural ability to grasp the kinds of knowledge and understanding they would need to oversee NASA's next generation of space shuttles or to manage the Federal Reserve or to lobby before Congress for gun control. But if college entry requires Elementary Physics or Introduction to Accounting or Qualitative Reasoning, I see no reason why any student, with enough personal effort and academic support, cannot fulfill these kinds of requirements reasonably well.

Throughout their education, your children will face countless experiences with failure, setbacks, disappointments, and discouragement. *This is not a bad thing.* This is the stuff of which resilience is made. It breaks my heart, too, to see that defeated look in my children's eyes, but we all need to keep *our* eyes on the larger vision we have for our children's futures. In short:

- ◉ Value your children's efforts, even if the outcome is not yet what you would like it to be.
- ◉ Emphasize the reality that things will not always go their way.
- ◉ Praise—don't pity—your children for having to work hard.

## Talking About Effort and Ability

If I try and try and try and try and try and try I'll get smarter and smarter and smarter and smarter and smarter and smarter.

—*Peter, four-year-old preschooler*

I'm dumb at math, and there's nothing I can do about it.

—*Helen, third grader*

Like Peter, the vast majority of young children from about four to six years of age believe very strongly that effort is the key to increasing intelligence. Most are delighted to learn new and challenging things in kindergarten and first grade, with little concern over any mistakes they might make or for how their friends are doing compared to them. Furthermore, they are delightfully positive about *everything* they are learning, from reading to writing to beginning arithmetic. Regrettably, this positive attitude about learning changes relatively quickly once schooling begins in earnest. By the end of first grade or the beginning of second grade, children begin to see the relationship between effort and ability completely differently, in a way that can only be described as *compensatory*. In other words, they now come to believe that the harder they *have* to try, the "dumber" they must be. For the first time, children perceive their ability as something that is limited by their intellectual *capacity*. When this realization sets in, effort becomes the proverbial double-edged sword that I referred to in Chapter One. By the fourth or fifth grade, children's evaluations of their own abilities in different areas become relatively stable, and they can readily identify subjects they are "good at" and "bad in."

The change in thinking between first and second grade does not happen by chance. It coincides with the onset of formal evaluations, about which children quickly become aware. Grades, report cards, reading group assignments, and the like heighten the natural desire that children have to know how they are doing relative to other students in their class. Once their interest is piqued, they become very good at knowing the "pecking order." Believe it or not, in relation to the teacher's evaluations, second graders can accurately rank-order themselves and the children in their classrooms according to who is the "smartest," the "next smartest," all the way down to the "least smart."

As much as we may wish that schools were more cooperative and less competitive, the reality is that the majority of our classrooms continue to be structured in the traditional way, with children marked on the basis of how they are doing relative to everyone else, not relative to how they have progressed over time. By definition, there can be only a few children at the top and bottom of the classroom, and most children fall somewhere in between. In order for your children to do well, someone else's children have to do poorly. In other words, they are learning in an environment in which the rewards, whatever they may be, are limited. Not surprisingly, classrooms in which comparisons between children are obvious make children much more self-conscious of their own abilities relative to those of their peers. In this kind of atmosphere, children become overly concerned with how "smart" they are relative to others, and this concern takes their focus away from the *process* and onto the *products* of learning. Many become oriented toward looking "smart," avoiding looking "dumb," and dodging work, especially challenging work.

Your job as a parent becomes ever more critical at this point. You cannot minimize your children's concerns over where they stand in the intellectual pecking order—their worries are real. Take, for example, this exchange:

> *Mara (third grader):* I'm so stupid.
> *Jim (her father):* No you're not!
> *Mara:* Yes I am! I never get all A's like Hannah does.
> *Jim:* Big deal. Hannah's not so great at everything, you

know. I've seen her out on the soccer field—
you're way better than her! And anyhow, you got
a good grade on your last medieval assignment.

*Mara:* Yeah, I really lucked out.

*Jim:* See! I told you so!

I doubt very much that, despite his good intentions, Jim has comforted his daughter in any genuine sense. He is denying what Mara knows to be true—that Hannah is an excellent student and a much better one than she is. To add insult to injury, Jim tries to make Mara feel better by pointing out how much better she is on the soccer field, a comparison that is inappropriate—apples and oranges, if you will. Mara's concerns are about her intellectual, not physical, abilities. And Jim does not pick up on a significant comment—that Mara thinks her recent good grade was the result of luck. Students who see luck as the cause of failure *or* success are treading on very dangerous ground, because they are holding the belief that they can have no control over how well or poorly they do in school. Now consider this exchange:

*Andrew:* I'm so stupid!

*Sam (his father):* Why do you say that?

*Andrew:* Because Max always gets A's on everything.
He's so much smarter than I am.

*Sam:* So you think you're stupid because Max always
gets A's?

*Andrew:* Well, duh, that's what I just said.

*Sam:* Lip from you, I don't need. So why do you think
Max always gets A's?

*Andrew:* Because he's really smart. Everything is so
easy for him—it's not fair. . . .

*Sam:* Did it ever occur to you that Max works harder
than you do? How many times in the past month
have you panicked because you realized you had a

big project due the next day? Do you think that
doing the work in a couple of desperate hours
might have something to do with the grades
you're getting?

*Andrew:* Maybe . . .

*Sam:* And what about the fabulous report you did on
Maya Angelou? Was that a stroke of luck?

*Andrew:* No way! I worked really hard on that one—
I even turned it in early, remember?

*Sam:* Ah . . . so instead of fussing about Max's A's,
maybe you can let us help you get organized so
every project goes as well as the poetry one.

*Andrew:* OK, OK already.

Notice how in this exchange Sam is focusing his son away from
his friend's grades and onto Andrew's own poor working habits. In
so doing, Sam is making him think about the reasons for his bad
grades, reasons that he emphasizes are entirely within his son's
control. He is also offering an opportunity to teach Andrew bank-
able strategies that can help him do better in the future. Sam's
approach does not apply only to situations in which children are
doing poorly. It is equally important to emphasize the process that
contributes to your children's *good* grades. Children who are doing
well in school also need to know that their performance is due
largely to elements within their control: their efforts, strategies, and
study habits.

Much of the educational research on the exemplary achievement of Asian students has focused on the fact that, relative to
American mothers and children, Japanese and Chinese mothers
and children place much more weight on effort than on ability in
explaining the causes of success and failure. This difference has led
many educational observers to argue that our tendency to focus on
innate ability is doing us in and that we should henceforth instruct
children that high achievement is within their reach, regardless of

whether they think they are smart or "dumb." As every teacher will tell you, children are not naive. They need to know and believe they have *some* intelligence, in order to invest effort in their learning. In other words, innate ability and intelligence are not dirty words. The key is to allow children to acknowledge their academic strengths and weaknesses and use these as jumping-off points for developing strategies for learning. Understanding the reasons for success and failure consumes a lot of our children's mental energy. As you will see in the list that follows, you can capitalize on your children's attempts to understand their grades and test scores in ways that will orient them toward positive beliefs about learning. In helping your children understand the reasons for the grades and other evaluations they receive,

- Focus on behavior over which they can exercise *control,* such as how much time they invest in a given project or assignment.
- Acknowledge the role of innate ability, *but . . .*
- Focus on strategies that can enhance their intelligence, making them "smarter."
- Focus on *purposeful* effort as a tool for getting to where they want to be.

## Talking About Success and Failure

All of us have a very natural need to understand the reasons why we succeed or fail on a particular task, project, or assignment. Children are no different. A satisfying grade makes every child happy, as much as a poor one makes children sad and disappointed. Beyond these general emotions lies a complex reasoning system that has a profound influence on how children come to think about the relationship between effort and ability and, ultimately, their own intelligence.

Think back to Mara, whose discussion with her father appeared earlier in this chapter. She thinks she's stupid in virtually everything. To boot, when she does get a good grade, she thinks it is because she "lucked out." From her perspective, it probably makes little or no sense to try—she just doesn't have the ability to do well, and her father's well-intentioned attempt to make her feel better gives her no other way of thinking about why she is doing poorly. Perhaps her father, who knows how well Hannah and some of the other children are doing in Mara's class, also thinks Mara really does not measure up—we just don't know.

We *do* know, however, that Andrew's father thinks Andrew has the ability to do well. In his father's mind, Andrew has no one to blame but himself for his lousy grades because he almost always sees fit to start his work at the last possible minute. I don't worry about a boy like Andrew. He may drive his parents crazy, but they are working on getting him to see that his performance in school is due partly to his ability, largely to his efforts (or lack of them, as is currently the case), and not at all to any external factors, such as luck. Without realizing it, Andrew's father is planting the seeds of resiliency in his son. He is guiding Andrew toward the realization that how well he does in school is pretty much a function of factors that are *within his control.*

I *do* worry about Mara, though. She thinks she is dumb and that any good grade she gets is the result of sheer luck. Her father is unwittingly reinforcing her belief by not guiding her away from it. To Mara's way of thinking, there is no point in studying harder or preparing further in advance for a test. The chances of her becoming the kind of student who can tolerate difficulty and challenge is minimal.

Now consider the concerns of the following three mothers, all of whom are dealing with what appear to be completely irrational children. Nancy describes her predicament with her teenager:

> I'm going out of my mind. No matter how much we
> talk to Jason [an eighth grader] or try to punish him,

he still waits until the last minute to study for tests.
Then he flies into a wild panic, and we all go crazy.
He knows he's the kind of kid who needs lots of lead
time to prepare. The result of all this is that he is a
very mediocre student. This has been going on for
years. I have no idea what to do.

Of course Jason knows that he stands a much better chance of
doing well if he studies ahead of time. What he *believes*, however,
is a different story altogether. He is convinced that he has been incredibly lucky so far—some of the tests have been hard, and on
these he has not done well. Others, though, have been really easy,
so he is not failing. What if he starts to prepare for tests the way his
parents say he should and then does poorly? All the time and effort
he would have invested will confirm what he senses: that he is just
not smart enough. In his mind, it makes more sense to continue to
take chances and hope that his luck holds out. When he gets a bad
grade, he's better off blaming it on the fact that he did not study
enough. After all, although he might not fail, he is afraid that he
can indeed do poorly even if he studies; it is better to fail for not
having studied than for not being smart.

Sophie has a different but related concern:

It breaks my heart. Julie [a seventh grader] studies
hard and well for every single math test. Then I get
them back, and they are packed full of unbelievably
careless errors. I've talked with her about checking
over her work before the teacher collects it, but it
seems to go in one ear and out the other. I'm beside
myself.

Contrary to her parent's beliefs, Julie does not believe she gets
bad grades because she makes careless mistakes. She believes that

she gets bad grades because she is dumb. In her mind, it won't make a bit of difference whether or not she checks over her work. She doesn't have what it takes (in other words, the intelligence) to spot her errors. Now consider Heidi's problem with her son:

> You think you've got it bad? Matt [a ninth grader] deliberately chooses science projects that are far and away below what he is capable of doing. I've talked until I'm blue in the face—what the heck is going on?

Matt is indeed a very smart guy. He has cleverly devised a strategy that will almost always guarantee success. He knows he is smart in science, but he also believes that, compared to others, he is not *that* smart. Choosing projects that he knows he can complete easily and well avoids the anxiety that comes from challenging himself. In his mind, he is much better off ensuring good grades, even if he doesn't learn anything, than risking a bad grade for the sake of learning something new.

In Nancy's case, it is clear that *something* has to be done about Jason's tendency to wait until the last minute to study for tests. In light of the fact that discussion and punishment have not made a difference, his parents need to take control, at least temporarily. One strategy open to them is to work closely with the teachers. For example, they could design a two-month trial period during which they make sure they know when a test is scheduled. Armed with this information, they can set up a study schedule with Jason. At this point, he may be the type of student who needs to have a parent sit and review material with him, quizzing him along the way. His parents would essentially become models for how to study. This idea requires a tremendous commitment of time from his parents, both of whom work. Yet it is a plan that holds promise for Jason. The hope is that, over time, he would slowly let go of his belief that luck will (or will not) pull him through. Naturally, his parents are aware that this will not happen overnight.

Sophie could begin by sitting Julie down and having her do all the problems on the math test that she got wrong. The goal would be for Julie to recognize her errors as what they are: careless. Sophie could ask Julie to talk aloud through each missed problem, noting where she thinks she went wrong. As Julie goes through each one, Sophie could be there to point out whatever careless mistakes Julie overlooks. Like Nancy, Sophie would be modeling strategies for how to double-check tests before Julie turns them in. It is hoped that it would not take Julie a long time to realize that she really *has* been finishing her tests too quickly.

Heidi has an altogether different problem with Matt. Like Nancy, she needs to enlist the aid of the teacher. She could work out a plan with the science teacher in which Matt would be required to turn in an abstract of his project idea prior to beginning his work. The teacher could then alter the proposed project in ways that would make it more challenging. I doubt that Matt would be happy about all this, and Heidi knows that she will have to work with any fallout that ensues.

In each of these examples you can see the powerful influence that children's beliefs about effort and ability have on their learning and motivation. The maddening thing for us as parents and for our children's teachers is that these three students are perfectly capable of doing good work—they just don't believe this to be the case. Their academic strategies are quite rational to them.

Every conversation about grades and report cards is an opportunity to convey ideas about effort and ability that can help your children build stronger study skills and become better students. By all means capitalize on all the opportunities that come your way, for it is in every conversation, big or small, that you can plant a seed of resilience against future hardships:

- Acknowledge your children's tendencies to compare themselves with their peers, yet downplay the importance of intelligence per se in good grades.
- Avoid empty platitudes such as "You just need to try harder."

◉ Emphasize that purposeful effort—effort that is planned—will make all the difference in improving study skills and therefore grades.

◉ Disabuse your children of the notion that they can count on luck to pull them through.

◉ At the same time, let them know that bad luck or not being the teacher's pet has nothing to do with how poorly they are doing in school.

◉ Keep your children from ruminating endlessly about a bad grade. Focus their attentions on learning from their mistakes and moving forward to prepare for the next test or assignment.

## Talking to Girls About Success and Failure

As I mentioned earlier in this chapter, many people assume that "smarter" children have no problems motivating themselves to do the great work that they do. But, in fact, it is frequently the "smarter" students, and particularly the "smarter" *girls*, who are unsure of their abilities, do not expect that they will do well in school, and shy away from challenging work for fear of making mistakes.

Nowhere is this more apparent than in the performance of boys and girls in mathematics. Girls do much better than boys in math, especially in elementary school. By middle and high school, these differences even out. Even though girls are equal or superior to boys in math performance, they are less confident than boys about their math abilities. Compared to boys, they do not believe they can be as successful. By high school, girls opt out of higher-level math and science courses at much greater rates than boys. To be sure, this has a domino effect on girls' college major and career choices. For example, young women are very much absent from departments of science and engineering across the nation.

Educators, psychologists, and even biologists have been exploring this problem for some time, but one thing is sure: we explain success and failure in math very differently to boys than we do to girls. We send very different messages about what it takes to succeed. In many studies of mothers' beliefs about the causes of success and failure in mathematics, mothers of boys overwhelmingly attribute their sons' success to high ability; in other words, they are "smart" in math. These same mothers argue that poor or failing grades from their boys are largely the result of lack of effort. Ask the same questions of mothers of girls, and the explanations are quite different. According to these mothers, girls' success in math is largely due to high effort: they try hard. When they do poorly, it is because they are not smart enough in math: they lack the ability to excel.

The messages are subtle but powerful. Boys are being implicitly told that their high performance is due to their innate intelligence—something stable they will always be able to count on. Where failure is concerned, the reason points squarely at lack of effort, something that is entirely within their control. In other words, not only are they smart, but they also have the power to turn failure into success. Where girls are concerned, however, the message is quite the inverse. The good news is that they are hearing about the importance of effort in achievement. The bad news is that they hear about their lack of innate ability to do exemplary work. Is it any wonder, then, that when students have more latitude in course choices, it is girls and not boys who shy away from advanced courses in science and mathematics?

This difference in attitudes is probably hard for many of you to hear about, especially in an era when gender equity in education is an issue so much at the forefront of national debates on school reform. The most open-minded parents cannot believe they communicate such different messages to their boys and girls, yet many of them do. Be mindful of how you help your boys and girls understand the reasons for success and failure in *all* subjects, for we tend to think that girls are better—more able—in language arts.

This caution extends to how you characterize each of your children. Many students tell me that they are the "artistic" or "athletic" or "funny" ones in the family and that another sibling is the "smart" one. Your children are bound to differ from one another in their skills in different arenas, and they are bound to realize this from a relatively early age. Of course, none of us intends to offend our children when we identify them in these ways. In fact, these characterizations are often cute and become part of your family's lore. Yet by definition they are limiting in the sense that they imply that the "athletic" child cannot also be the "smart" child. Goodness knows, this is the last thing any of us intends to communicate.

- ◉ Do not turn your children's strengths into labels.
- ◉ Enlist your children to teach one another, whatever the skill.
- ◉ Let your children know that their *ability* is the foundation for learning, but that only *effort* will make them smarter.

## What to Do When Sustained Effort Yields Little Improvement

I'm sick of this! I go for extra help, I do extra problems, I go over all my tests with Mr. Smith, and my folks even got me a tutor. I'm just not getting any better at trig. It's driving me crazy, and I hate it, hate it, hate it!

—*Ethan, tenth grader*

I wish I could say that purposeful effort, combined with a serious commitment to learning, will guarantee high achievement for all students. Regrettably, there are times when students put a great deal of effort into their learning and find that they continue to have difficulties. These periods, such as the one experienced by Ethan, are very trying for parents and their children. Some subjects simply do not come easily to a lot of students, and it would be naive to think that effort can turn any low achiever into a stellar student.

In these situations you need to sit back and reevaluate your student's goals. Ethan has shown his parents that he is doing the best he can, and he is indeed working to his maximum. In his case, he has to have trigonometry on his high school transcript, and he has no choice but to suffer through it. His parents are supporting his efforts in the best ways they know how. Collectively they have decided that this is one of those times when Ethan just has to be miserable, as his father Robert explains:

> Listen, Ethan, this trig business is awful. Your Mom and I have a lot of admiration for you—for how hard you are working and for how tough it is for you to get grades you're not used to getting. The point is that this is the only time in your life you will be taking a course like this. We all just have to grin and bear it. We have no other choice. I know you'll make it— you may not get an A, but you will pass, and that's all you need.

Notice how Robert expresses not pity but respect for his son's efforts. At this point, he is putting the best face possible on an eminently difficult experience. He is allowing his son to feel angry and frustrated, and letting him know he has confidence that Ethan will meet the overall goal of passing the course. Robert accepts, and is allowing Ethan to accept, that an A in trigonometry may very well be outside Ethan's reach, but that that is OK. In other words, in the context of the quality of Ethan's other work and of the requirements he needs to fulfill for college admission, Robert is acknowledging that Ethan is doing the very best he can and that it will suffice.

In fact, Robert and his family are in much better shape for being realistic than Corey, a student of mine some years ago who was bound and determined to attend medical school. At the time I met him, he had been enrolled in night school for three years in preparation for his ultimate goal. My admiration quickly turned to concern when I learned that he had failed every entrance requirement at least two or three times. Corey remained remarkably optimistic and committed to repeating anatomy, biochemistry, and biology until he passed. Effort is indeed a virtue, but like anything in its extreme, it can be debilitating. There may come a time when your student should reevaluate his or her goals.

- Be realistic and truthful with yourself about your child's difficulties.
- Encourage the same realism and truthfulness in your child.
- Do not offer your child pity—offer alternative strategies instead.
- Recognize that it is a gift to know "when to say when."
- Focus on learning as a *process*, and *effort* as the means to learn.
- Show pride in your children's *progress*: focus their attentions on how their knowledge and understanding has grown over time.

As I have mentioned throughout this chapter, our beliefs, whatever they may be, lead us to say and do certain specific things with regard to our children's education. In turn, the things we say and do have a profound effect on our children's developing beliefs about how smart they are and what it takes to do well in school. In the next chapter, I talk about how you can capitalize on everyday common occurrences to communicate helpful messages about learning and understanding.

# CHAPTER 3

# Supporting Achievement at Home

I love to bake, and I want my kids to enjoy it too. They really get into it. Bobby [ten] reads the recipe and breaks the eggs, Allison [twelve] measures out the dry and wet ingredients, and Danny [eight] mixes the batter. I have to tell you, though, that what takes me a half hour to do takes all of us about an hour and a half. By the time I've fished eggshells out of the batter and wiped batter off the walls and ceiling, I'm done in. It really is a lot of fun, though.

—*Leslie, mother of three*

The great majority of parents are completely unaware of the millions of ways that they support academic achievement at home. Leslie would probably be surprised to learn that in involving her children in baking their favorite cake she is reinforcing essential elements of language and reading acquisition, as well as rudimentary aspects of mathematics, including measurement and estimation. Clearly this is not the reason she and her children bake together; they just love creating something delicious that they can devour as soon as it is cooled and iced.

There is no one prescription for supporting your children's achievement at home that will guarantee success in school. There are as many ways to encourage academic excellence as there are parents and children. You are the best judge of what works for you, your family, and each of your children. The simple, everyday activities that parents engage in with their children, such as putting away the groceries or playing a board game, may seem straightforward to the outsider but are actually rather complex tasks that can, at times, pose problems for many parents. When children experience some uncertainty about where the packages of macaroni and cheese belong, or what the rules of the game say about turn-taking, you need to step in to provide tips or pointers. In so doing, you may behave in ways that are well intentioned and in the best interests of the children, but sometimes your actions can actually pose greater problems. For example, when your children are stuck, should you offer assistance right away, or should you wait to see if they can figure out a solution? If you decide to wait, how long should you wait: a minute, or five minutes, or until your children ask for help? What if your child is the type who doesn't like to ask for help— what then? Should you offer it at some point anyway? There are no easy or pat answers to questions such as these. What parents choose to do will vary according to the particular situation. The point is that, despite your best efforts, you may make mistakes or not necessarily be able to predict the consequences of your actions for your children's learning. Our discussions in this chapter will prepare us to tackle the sometimes painful topic I speak about in Chapter Four: dealing with your children's homework.

## Encouraging Your Children's Intellectual Abilities

Many parents believe that the best way to foster their children's intellectual development is to expose them to a variety of stimulating experiences that will open their minds to different ways of seeing, thinking, and knowing. Fueled perhaps by concerns that their children are growing up in a society—indeed a world—that is so much more fast paced and competitive than the one in which they grew up, a great many parents have taken to the general, unfounded assumption that "earlier is better."

In fact, there is quite a growth industry catering to parents who are anxious for their children to "get a leg up" on everyone else's children before they begin kindergarten. For example, Glenn Doman's Better Baby Institute claims that in one short (and expensive) week, he and his colleagues can help you teach your *baby* to read. The titles of his popular books say it all: *Teach Your Baby Math, How to Multiply Your Baby's Intelligence,* and *How to Give Your Baby an Encyclopedic Mind* all promise to show you how you can make your baby "smarter" than everyone else's. None of these efforts are necessary, and they place too much pressure on children at a very early age. Although most parents do not go to such extremes, many nonetheless feel the need to expose their children to new and exciting experiences on a regular basis.

> I've run out of things to do on weekends. My kids
> hate the children's museum, and they're bored with
> the science museum, the aquarium, and the zoo. I
> tell you, the weekends are getting stressful because
> the kids are bored and want to go somewhere new
> and do something special. I comb the weekly listings
> in the newspaper for ideas of where to take them,
> but I'm all out of ideas.
>
> —*Angela, mother of a*
> *four-year-old and six-year-old*

Angela is exhausting herself for no good reason. Her children would have been just as happy to go to the park and get an ice cream cone afterwards. Unfortunately, she has set a precedent that is much more trouble than it is worth, and the result is that her children are bored at a very young age with activities that thrill most youngsters who are exposed to them at a later age and with less frequency. In other words, for Angela's boys, the special occasion has become old hat. What makes Angela's dilemma unfortunate is that there are countless rich and rewarding learning experiences that are embedded in her children's everyday life—she just doesn't recognize them because they are so very ordinary. But it is in the ordinary that our children learn the basics of early reading and numerical thinking. Take your children on your weekly trip to the grocery store, ask them to set the table, have them help with the laundry. Mundane? Yes, of course, but no less stimulating, and probably more of a learning experience for young children than a schlep to your city's museums.

Bear with me while I ask you to think about all the steps you take when you go shopping for food. You may first make a shopping list of things you need. When you arrive at the store, you procure a shopping cart and begin your trek down the aisles, most likely in the same way each time. As you proceed down each aisle, you choose items for your basket (and put back others that your children surreptitiously slip in), perhaps crossing each item off your list as you find it. Along the way, you use different methods to select the things you need. For example, you buy onions by the bag, but you select your peaches individually. You check apples and bananas for bruises, celery for crispness, milk for the expiration date, eggs for cracks. Finally, when you are done, you proceed to the checkout counter, where every item is scanned and bagged, and you pay for your purchases.

Back home, everything needs to be put away. In your (relatively) organized kitchen and pantry, everything has its place. The canned goods belong in the cupboard next to the fridge. In this cupboard, the canned fruits are on the left, and the canned vegetables on the right. Spices go in your spice drawer. Eggs, milk, and fresh fruits and vegetables go in their appropriate shelves and bins in the refrigerator; frozen waffles and ice cream belong in the freezer. Paper towels go under your sink. Bathroom tissues go in your linen closet. Laundry detergent goes in the laundry basket.

When you involve your children in each of these tasks that make up the activity of "grocery shopping," you are implicitly teaching them how to select among a wide variety of items that your family needs, how to judge freshness, and when to know that the family may need more than the usual amount of any given item (for example, if guests are coming for dinner). By the time your children have finished helping you put everything away, you will have taught them, implicitly, how to categorize objects by type (food and non-food), class within type (canned, fresh, frozen), group within class (vegetable or fruit), size (large versus small cans), location (large cans in the back, small cans in the front), and even color. ("The yellow can has pineapple in it. The red can has kidney beans in it.") Week after week, month after month, without your even realizing it, you have "taught" your children that things belong in categories and that items within categories are nested and can be combined. In other words, your children will have soaked up all manner of knowledge about classification that involves everyday items they see and use in their lives.

None of us ever makes a point of teaching our children how grocery stores are organized, yet each trip down the grocery aisles constitutes a "lesson" in organization. Children learn quickly that items are not randomly distributed on shelves. There is the cereal aisle, the bread aisle, the juice aisle, and so on. It will eventually dawn on them that larger items are on the bottom shelves and smaller ones on the upper shelves, and that fresh fruits, vegetables, meat, and dairy ring the perimeter of the store. And your children will realize, in their own ways, that you can't walk out of the store without giving somebody something called money. Sometimes you get some back, sometimes you don't. Sometimes you hand over bills and coins, sometimes only bills, sometimes lots of bills, sometimes only one or two. Whatever the amount, the person at the checkout is always reciting numbers. Over time, these observations lend themselves to children's realization that the numbers are associated with how much things cost and that the counting is related to the bills and coins you have handed over.

This virtual trip to the store and putting the groceries away at home shows you just how much teaching and learning goes on in "normal" everyday life. Now think about everything else you and your partner do to maintain your household—tidying up, cleaning, cooking and baking, doing the laundry—and you gain an even greater sense of the rich intellectual environment you are providing for your children. You do not need to schedule learning in your children's lives. It occurs in subtle and indirect ways. It even happens in spite of you.

- ❧ Let your children help you do things around your home.
- ❧ Specifically, give your children "jobs" to do, such as pouring laundry detergent into the washing machine.
- ❧ Take your children with you when you run your regular errands—to the grocery store, the bank, the dry cleaner, and the post office.

## Helping Your Children Acquire New Skills

From showing our children how to put groceries away to teaching them how to tie their shoes to helping them learn to read, much of our time with our children is spent teaching them how to master new skills and become effective learners. Exactly *how* we go about doing this is the subject of a great many studies of parents and their children. One thing is clear: although there is no one best way to take on this daunting responsibility, some strategies are better suited than others for guiding children's intellectual development.

Ideally, your children will be best prepared to meet the demands of their teachers if they are *active* and not passive learners. In other words, our schools call on children to be inquisitive, think independently, and take initiative in their own learning. To harken back to our discussions in Chapter Two, their development into active learners depends very much on the degree to which you will have allowed them to explore, make mistakes, and learn that there are multiple ways to arrive at the same solution, whether the problem involves filling in the missing vowels in a list of words, serving "tea" at a party, building a Lego bridge strong enough to hold an army of knights, or drawing a cat on their Etch-a-Sketch.

To be sure, there is a limit to how much we can and should let our children flounder. We need to be there to provide assistance *when it is necessary*. Herein lies the rub—one parent's decision to back off parallels another's decision to plunge in. How can we know when we are intervening too much—or too little, for that matter? As you might expect, there is no easy answer. The overall goal is to get your children to progress from clueless novice to accomplished expert, and to foster active rather than passive learning along the way. Here is an excerpt from an interaction between Jessica and her five-year-old son, John, while they were putting groceries away:

> *Jessica:* OK, you put all the cans in the pantry while I unpack the rest of the bags.
>
> *John (proudly):* All done!
>
> *Jessica:* Honey, that's really nice, but it's not quite right.
>
> *John:* Yeah, it is. The small ones are on one shelf, and the big ones are on the other. That way we can see them.
>
> *Jessica:* Yes, honey, that's true. But look: you mixed up the fruit cocktail with the corn and peas. Here, let me do it so you can see . . . There, that looks better, doesn't it? Wait a second—why in the world did you put the milk in here?
>
> *John:* Because it goes great with the Oreos.
>
> *Jessica:* For heaven's sake—it'll go bad! You know that! Put it in the fridge, OK? OK, can you put the Goldfish and Wheat Thins away now?
>
> *John:* Yeah, just show me where they go.

Jessica's style is to be very directive. She asks John for his help, criticizes his method, and then does the job herself. It is very important for Jessica that things get put away just where she likes them to be. This is not lost on John, who is quick to ask his mother where the next items should go. It doesn't take long for him to realize that there is a right way (his mother's) and a wrong way to put groceries away. Compare this with Laurie's approach to teaching Roxy to do the same thing:

*Laurie:* OK, Roxy, let's get everything out of the bags first. OK, what should we put in the pantry?

*Roxy:* The milk and the Oreos.

*Laurie:* Why?

*Roxy:* Because they go together, silly!

*Laurie:* That's true. But why not put the ice cream in too? It goes great with Oreos.

*Roxy:* Mom! The ice cream will melt—everybody knows that!

*Laurie:* Oh, OK. But don't we always put the milk in the fridge?

*Roxy:* Yeah, so?

*Laurie:* Well, if the ice cream will melt in the pantry, the milk will go bad in the pantry. They're both dairy products; they need to be kept cold.

*Roxy:* Oh yeah, I forgot. So let's put the Oreos in the fridge with the milk!

*Laurie:* We can do that if we want to, but let's wait and see if there's room, OK? Which cans do you think belong together on the same shelf?

*Roxy:* The short ones.

*Laurie:* You mean we should put the short ones on one shelf and the tall ones on another?

*Roxy:* Yeah, that way we can see them better.

*Laurie:* That's a great idea! What about another way?

let them figure things out & make mistakes before providing answers.
(even let them devise new systems of doing things)

*Roxy:* We could put the reddish-pinkish cans on one
    shelf and the bluish-greenish cans on the other.
*Laurie:* I like that idea! Which one do *you* prefer?
*Roxy:* Reddish-pinkish and bluish-greenish.
*Laurie:* OK, go ahead then, and I'll get the stuff in the
    fridge.
*Roxy:* Don't forget the Oreos!

Notice how Laurie is sensitive enough to realize that for Roxy, milk and Oreos belong in the same category and so should be put away in the same place. Rather than criticizing Roxy outright for putting the milk in the pantry, Laurie guides her thinking so that she realizes herself that it must go in the fridge. And, for now, it matters nothing at all to Laurie that Roxy will place sweet and savory items on the same shelf.

Also important is that Laurie is pushing Roxy to think about more than one way to categorize cans of food. Rather than criticizing Roxy's ideas, Laurie shows her that she is delighted with the options Roxy has come up with. I'm sure Laurie is less than delighted about having the cans sorted by color—that obviously is not her method of choice. But her preference matters much less to her than getting Roxy to conceptualize multiple solutions to one problem—that of putting groceries away. In this context, she bites her tongue and lets her daughter know that there is no one "right" way to get food from the bag into the pantry. Given Laurie's openness, Roxy may very well experiment with different ways to store canned goods in the pantry. I doubt that John will feel free to do the same.

Quite unbeknownst to Jessica and Laurie, parents play a vital role in organizing the introduction of new tasks to children, keeping a constant check on the difficulty level at each step toward the solution, supplying hints at appropriate places, and perhaps most important, modeling strategies for their children when they get "stuck." In essence, whenever you teach your children to do something new, you are finding ways to use what is familiar to them to help them make sense of the unfamiliar.

Imagine teaching your children how to do a puzzle for the first time. Initially, you guide your children step by step toward the solution. Very slowly, as they "get the hang of it," you back off little by little, until they are doing the task entirely on their own. In other words, we act much like a scaffold on a building, providing a lot of support in the beginning and gradually "dismantling" our help as our children become more familiar with the puzzle. Depending on the task, some children will need more help than others in their progression from novice to expert. Some might catch on right away; others will need more time. That is to say, we will take down our scaffold of assistance earlier for some than for others.

Ideally, we choose puzzles, problems, or physical activities that are neither too easy nor too hard. For example, there would be no point in keeping a ten-year-old on the baby hill after her first season of skiing. Her progress will be such that she can progress to more challenging slopes. And although this child has mastered the rudiments of the sport, it would be nothing short of pure folly to take the same girl up the chairlift to descend the most difficult mountain. Small but challenging steps toward mastery are what this girl needs. And, as every ski instructor will tell you, she needs to fall in order to learn how to get up and how to minimize injuries. Past a certain, relatively early point, her instructor would never dream of catching her before she falls—doing so would defeat the purpose altogether.

As another example, there would be no point in keeping a five-year-old busy with chunky block puzzles that contain no more than ten pieces. Her progress is such that she can move on to more and more challenging puzzles. And although she has mastered the rudiments of putting a puzzle together, it would be entirely inappropriate to give her a three-hundred-piece 3-D puzzle of Big Ben. Small but challenging steps toward mastery are what this girl needs. And, as every teacher will tell you, she needs to struggle a bit in order to learn to put a somewhat larger puzzle together. Past a certain, relatively early point, her teacher would never dream of having the child watch while the teacher completes the puzzle herself—doing so would defeat the purpose altogether.

And so it is with intellectual tasks, although many of us do not see them the same way. This might be because we can *see* physical progress more readily than academic progress. When we watch our children miss the jump shot, fall off their bikes, or trip up on their roller blades, we understand the absolute necessity of these setbacks for their ultimate ability to master the particular skill. With schooling, it is very hard to watch our children become confused and frustrated. We worry that experiences like these will make them lose interest in learning. We certainly don't want their desire to learn to suffer, so it is with the best of intentions that we dole out the hints or provide the answer outright (much like Jessica putting the cans away herself). In short, we keep them from failing.

Ultimately the issue comes down to one of *control.* Ironically, when we try to control too much of our children's learning experiences, we end up depriving them of the very opportunities we want them to have. Furthermore, we end up communicating ideas about learning that we never intended to convey, and quite unwittingly we make our children anxious about making mistakes. Take, for example, the following exchange, of which I was a part some time ago. Mary was two-and-a-half years old when she invited me to "tea." She set the little table with a tablecloth, napkins, cookie platter, and, of course, the plastic teapot and teacups. She served me "cookies" and prepared to pour the "tea" from an empty play teapot:

> *Mary:* Do you want some tea now?
>
> *Janine:* Oh yes, please.
>
> *Mary:* OK, put your cup on top of the spout, and I'll pour.
>
> *Janine:* OK, here it is.
>
> *Jared (Mary's father):* Sweetie, that's not how you pour

tea! It would spill and make a mess. Put the
teacup back on the saucer, put the saucer back
down on the table, and *then* pour the tea from the
spout *into* the cup.

Mary started over and poured the tea correctly. This is a rather
trivial incident, but it nonetheless reveals that there are many
times when it is of little value to control children's pretend play.
None of us would doubt that when the time comes for this child
to pour real tea from a porcelain teapot, she will do it properly. In
the meantime, however, her father has unwittingly made her concerned about playing tea party the right way.

Repeated attempts to make sure our children do things the
"right" way convey that there is only one way to solve problems.
This makes them anxious about making mistakes and about whether
they are doing things the right way. This is how Jessica and Jared
both are pushing their children to be passive learners.

Consider, instead, how Elena managed her four-year-old son's
mess when he poured her a *real* cup of tea:

> *Ted:* I wanna pour, I wanna pour!
> *Elena:* OK, be careful, go slowly because it's hot.
> *Ted:* I got it, I got it . . .
> *Elena (with half the tea in the saucer and the other half in*
> *her cup):* Good job!

For Elena, the mess is unimportant when compared with how
proud it makes her son feel to pour tea for her. Clearly, Ted did not
pour the tea the "right" way, but given a few more opportunities, he
will, and in the process he will have tuned his fine motor skills and
picked up some informal knowledge of liquid physics.

You need to have faith that, provided you involve your children in your daily and weekly routines, you are stocking their pool

of learning with a great many rich and stimulating experiences that will capitalize on their informal knowledge of language and mathematics. In other words, you know what you are doing—you just aren't terribly aware that you are doing it. Let your children be your guides. They will let you know what they are interested in, what they want to learn more about. Then step back, but not too far back, and let them learn from you and from their mistakes.

- ◉ Encourage pretend play and let your children set the rules.
- ◉ Do not question the wisdom of your children's rules, but rather ask your children to explain the reasons for their rules.

## Helping Your Children Develop into Mature Learners

Allow me to paint for you a portrait of a mature learner. Lily is twelve years old, and she loves to learn new things. She is happily relieved when something comes easily to her, but she really enjoys the challenge of mastering something hard in school, especially if she knows it is above her grade level. Yet, at the same time, she hates it when she doesn't understand something right away. She gets frustrated and angry with herself and turns to her mother or father for help. Unfortunately, by that point, her frustration level is so high that every well-intentioned suggestion is nothing short of "stupid." She eventually bursts into tears and runs to her room sobbing about the unfairness of it all.

After some time, she emerges from the safety of her room a transformed child. Bursting with ideas and strategies for solving the problem in question, she grabs a pile of scrap paper and asks a parent to sit with her while she talks through her ideas and sorts out one or more possible answers. Her parents sit, dumbfounded by the gamut of emotions they have observed, and wonder how they are going to survive her high school years.

At first glance, this peek into an evening of homework with Lily might lead one to believe that she is anything *but* a mature learner. Frustration, anger, and tears of hopelessness are not what most people would point to as signs of sophisticated and reasoned approaches to learning. Yet look at her behavior *after* her outburst, and you see all the qualities that teachers try so hard to foster: a willingness to try new and difficult things, genuine excitement in the process of rooting out a solution, and acceptance of the fact that there may be multiple ways to arrive at this solution.

I describe Lily to you in this way because I do not want you to think that children who are mature learners are necessarily exemplars of mature behavior. Her reaction to difficulty reflects the normal frustration of any young (or old) learner. After all, who among us loves to feel lost and completely confused? There is inherently nothing wrong with falling apart, as long as you know how to recover. This is where Lily demonstrates that she is indeed a mature learner—in her behavior *after* she has calmed herself down.

Helping your children to become resilient in the face of difficulties and setbacks is one of the greatest gifts you can give them. It is painful but true that our experiences are not always as easy as we would like, that we experience disappointment when we least expect it, and that things do not always go our way. All of us know how very difficult it can be to bounce back from setbacks and disappointment. And all of us have acquaintances or friends who have enormous problems coping with difficulty. They may ruminate over a disappointing experience for what seems like an eternity, all the while wasting precious time and energy that could otherwise be devoted to moving forward.

One thing is clear: the ability to withstand the frustrations of childhood, academic and otherwise, depends very much on having repeated encounters with these frustrations. Week after week, month after month, year after year, children *must* experience what it feels like to fail the test, to be left out when the party invitations get mailed, to be cut from the team, to succumb to someone else's schedule of when and how certain things can be done. These experiences during the childhood and adolescent years serve as the training ground for the development of resiliency. Here is where we parents come in, armed with a great deal of patience and a strong cup of coffee.

The skills that go into studying for a test or doing a project are varied, and they do not come easily to many children. When you realize how much more complicated schoolwork becomes as children get older, you appreciate the need to help your children develop these skills as soon as teachers begin to assign homework. From the first grader's math worksheet to the twelfth grader's critical essay on the economic restructuring of postcommunist Poland, students need to develop a reserve of strategies that will help them get their work done. Do not be lulled into thinking that your first grader's worksheet should be easy for him to complete. In fact, it is as complicated for him as the essay is for the twelfth grader.

Your children need to learn a variety of study skills in order to successfully complete their assignments, whatever these may be. And you need to help them learn these skills, which do not come naturally to a great many students. Show your children how to break down their homework into manageable pieces. Your confused first grader might find the worksheet more palatable if you literally conceal every question but the one he is working on. Doing so may keep him from being distracted by everything else that is yet to be done.

As for your twelfth grader, who among us wouldn't collapse at the mere thought of such a daunting essay? The work becomes much less panic inducing when we work with her *well before the assignment is due* to make a list of everything she needs to do before beginning to write: go to the library; gather references; take notes; make an basic outline, then a detailed outline; concentrate on and write one section at a time; read the entire essay for grammar, spelling, and flow of arguments. These complex tasks will be less intimidating if, over the years, you have helped your children gradually develop the skills they need to tackle such assignments, if not with confidence then at least with the knowledge that they know what they need to do and how they can get started.

- Infuse your home with a structure of predictable rules for when and how schoolwork needs to be done, and make your children's schooling your top priority.
- Steadfastly stand by your rules.
- Be prepared to deal with argumentative comparisons.
- Show young children how to break down their homework into manageable pieces.
- Teach older children how to use a time line to pace themselves.
- Find the proper balance between free-flowing permissiveness and rigid authoritarianism.

## Being (Reasonably) Involved in Your Children's Schooling

Parent involvement comes in many shapes and sizes. Although there is no "best" way to be involved in your children's education, certain messages do indeed make a difference. During their pre-school years, prepare them to become students. Speak in positive ways about the purpose of schooling and all that they will gain from the experience. Looking back to the discussion earlier in this chapter, emphasize the active role they must play in learning. For example, instead of telling your children that school is a place where they must sit quietly and listen to the teacher, let them know that school is a place where they will learn new things and get to ask many questions about how things work.

When your children begin school, get to know their teachers. These women and men need to know that you are interested in what they are doing and what your children are learning. Make every effort to go to parent-teacher conferences. In consideration of parents' hectic schedules, most teachers will meet with you early in the morning or in the evening. Teachers observe your children on a daily basis in a variety of academic, social, creative, and athletic situations. They have insights about your children that can help you understand their progress, both academically and socially. At the same time, you are a resource for teachers. You are in a unique position to share information that you think might help teachers better understand and teach your children.

Keep daily track of what your children are doing in school. Be aware of when assignments are due and when tests are scheduled, and help your children learn to prepare in advance. Do not feel that you need to be able to help with homework in order to help your children learn. Although it may seem counterintuitive, high-achieving students do not always have help from their parents. Many studies of high-achieving Indochinese and Latino students have shown that, although language barriers prevent many parents from being involved in a "hands-on" way, they encourage academic excellence in a variety of ways. For example, encourage your children to do their homework with one or more friends. In this way, you are ensuring a ready-made study group in which your children and their friends help one another with schoolwork. Or give your older children the responsibility of assisting and checking the work of your younger children.

Above all else, be wary of providing too much help. The balancing act of which I spoke earlier is a delicate one indeed. If your children are struggling but are not asking for assistance, leave them be. You do more harm than good by offering unsolicited help. Many children are surprised when adults step in unannounced and offer unsought or unwanted help. They assume that the adults believe they cannot do the work—that they are not smart enough. By trying to be nice, you will have unwittingly led your children to question their abilities. Do not "save" them from difficulty. Let them experience confusion and frustration, and be there to support their learning—to be their scaffold—when they seek you out.

I mentioned earlier that teachers are delighted to know that you are interested in and concerned about your children's education. Nonetheless, know your place. The last thing teachers want or need are parents who insist on giving advice or pointers on how or what to teach. If you are lucky enough to be able to volunteer an hour per week in your child's classroom, consider yourself as an aide—do whatever the teacher needs done. You are not there to monitor teachers' instructional styles. Believe it or not, managing parents can be an even harder task than managing children. To be sure, there may be times when you might have legitimate concerns about how your teacher is treating your child or what your teacher is teaching in the classroom. In cases such as these, you need to speak up and advocate for your child, and I will talk about these kinds of issues in Chapter Five.

## Helping Your Children Develop a Vision for Their Future

When Arcadia sophomore Johnson Lee gets home, his mother has vegetable sushi and eggrolls waiting on the kitchen table. When he stays up late—say, to cram with his friends over the Internet—she brews a pot of coffee to keep him going. And when there's just no room in his backpack for a hefty Advanced Placement biology textbook, no problem—she copies the chapters he needs on the machine outside his bedroom. In this household, failure is spelled B.

Up in Kern County, Taft Union High School student Dusty Watkins, the son of a petroleum company worker, wants to be a police officer or a game warden. Watkins, though, seldom does his homework—"It's boring." Sure, his father will ground him for nine weeks if he gets a shoddy grade. But what's a bad grade in this family? D.

Although we may not always be aware of it, the decisions we make and the efforts and worry that we put into raising our children help them develop a vision for what they can make of their future lives. And it is vital for our children, especially as they grow into adolescence, to develop a sense of their futures that reaches beyond the here and now. Think for a moment about how your teenager would finish this sentence: "My ultimate hope is that I will be able to . . ." Not surprisingly, students differ in how far into the future their completed statements take them. Some students write a sentence about the boy or girl they hope will be their date to the senior prom. Others compose a paragraph about their college and graduate school plans. Students who have a farther-reaching sense of their futures generally do better in school and are better adjusted than those whose future plans reach only into the near future.

Teenagers cannot develop a significant vision of their future overnight. It takes years to cultivate the knowledge and understanding that they will one day be responsible for themselves and their own families and that there is indeed a direct relationship between how well they do in school and the degree to which they will be able to fulfill their dreams. It is important to let your children know that, although they may be small, they have responsibilities that you expect them to fulfill. For example, when they are preschoolers, make sure they tidy up after themselves or help set the dinner table. When they begin kindergarten, make *them*, not you, responsible for dressing themselves and knowing where their backpack is. And when schoolwork begins in earnest, in the first grade, make it clear that, just as you and your partner have jobs to do, your children's *only* job is to do well in school. Your children need to know that inasmuch as you have obligations to them, to feed and clothe and house and love them, they have obligations to you. They need to take care of themselves more and more as they grow, and they need to be responsible learners.

- Have your children talk about what they imagine when they think about their futures, both short and long term.
- Encourage them to set goals for themselves.
- Discuss different ways in which they think they can attain their goals.
- Share information with your children about the skills they will need to reach their goals.

Many people often assume that because I study children's motivation to learn, I must have the answers to their burning questions: How do I motivate my child? What can I do to ensure high self-esteem? How can I make sure he understands that homework is essential to his learning? What's worse, many assume that because I "know so much," my children must be natural exemplars of motivated and excited learners. The truth is that we are all navigating in uncharted waters. We all support our children's achievement at home, in ways that are both purposeful and explicit, but more often in ways that are implicit and unspoken. We need to let our children be our guides and take our lead from them. They have their ways of letting us know what they are interested in, what they are struggling with, and how they want to learn. We have little to gain and much to lose when we try to orchestrate their learning experiences.

# CHAPTER 4

# Dealing with Homework

This homework thing is driving me crazy. All I
can tell you is that, when we were kids, we had
homework to do and we had to do it—no ifs,
ands, or buts. Nowadays, everything is open for
negotiation, from how much homework the teacher
should assign to when he should assign it to whether
it *really* needs to be done at all. I give up. . . .
— *Mother of third grader*

This homework thing is driving me crazy. I have
four kids, and all I do in the evening is supervise
homework. A lot of times, especially with my older
ones, the instructions aren't clear, and I have to
make two or three phone calls to other parents to
sort out what the assignment is all about. We have
no time as a family anymore, and I really resent it.
— *Mother of fifth grader*

For those of us with school-age children, the debate over homework
has become much like the debate over how and when toddlers
should be potty trained. Over time, we are exposed to the gamut of
opinions, whose staying power is inevitably limited. Most of us have

an intuitive sense that it is probably a good thing for our children to have homework. Beyond this general belief, it is very hard indeed to find common ground on the daily issues that homework presents. What is the goal of homework? Are there measurable, positive effects of homework? At what point should children have homework? How much should they have at different grade levels? How much is too much? Should parents be involved in their children's homework? If so, what should this involvement look like? Can parents be too involved? And what about everything else in our children's lives? Is there enough time for sports, music, art, community service, and plain-old hanging out at home, all of which are exceedingly important for children's psychological and social development? And why is the nation engaged in this debate in the first place?

Attitudes about homework have swung like the proverbial pendulum, from outright rejection to impassioned endorsement and back again. We are smack in the middle of heated public debates that have intensified during the 1990s. Not coincidentally, these arguments are running concurrently with the alarming knowledge that our children's academic achievement, especially in mathematics and science, lags well behind that of their peers in most other industrialized nations.

It is clear to me, as a parent and an educator, that homework has motivational benefits that far outweigh whatever academic advantages it may or may not possess. For some reason, these benefits, such as the ability to tolerate boredom, have not made it into the forum of public debate. I am not at all worried that our children may come to hate us, their teachers, and their schools. Let them vent their anger—that is a good thing. We do them no favors by feeling sorry for making them work hard. On the contrary, when we assign homework, we are giving them a gift on which they will be able to draw throughout their lives: the gift of our belief that they can accomplish things that seem, even to them, to be beyond their reach. In this chapter, I hope to show you just how valuable this gift can be in helping your children fulfill their dreams.

## The Backlash Against Homework

The parents quoted at the beginning of the chapter are expressing opinions about homework that represent a swing from one extreme to another. In the 1950s and 1960s, most parents would never have dreamed of questioning the teacher's judgment. In my own family, the teacher's word was law, and my parents did not tolerate any criticism of our teachers, ever. Homework, no matter how long or involved, was looked on as a very serious obligation. To question the teacher's pedagogy or, heaven forbid, to complain about the homework load was simply unheard of and tantamount to shameful disrespect for the teacher and the school. Yet today, as evidenced by the quotation that follows, we are engaged in a sort of collective lamentation over children's homework:

> There was blood, sweat, and a puddle of tears on kitchen tables across America this morning, the detritus of a long afternoon, stretching into evening, of yesterday's homework. . . . [Homework] is something that infuriates parents, sabotages family time, and crowds out so much else in a child's life.

In the early decades of this century, educators believed that homework was absolutely necessary to train the mind. For example, practice in rote memorization was considered to be essential for children's intellectual development. By the 1940s, educators shed this notion in favor of the growing belief that the goal of schooling was to develop children's abilities. At this point, homework was viewed as counterproductive to achieving this overall goal.

Then came the era of *Sputnik*. The Soviet launching of the first spacecraft in the 1950s caught politicians, scientists, and educators alike off guard. Educational public policy turned its spotlight on mathematics and science instruction and achievement, and homework was again seen as key to children's academic development and the nation's competitive survival. By the 1960s and 1970s, more liberal and easygoing ideas about schooling contributed to a backlash against competition in the classroom and the pressure on children to excel academically. According to some educational observers, public opinion looked more favorably on homework in the 1980s. I believe this was largely due to a convergence of two factors: at the same time that the American economy was doing very poorly relative to the Japanese economy, data on the underachievement of American as compared to Japanese students emerged.

As we sit at the cusp of the millennium, I am witness to a trend in which parents seem to reject homework and simultaneously demand higher academic standards in our public schools. At best, many parents today, especially children of the baby-boom era, are terribly ambivalent about homework for their children. They want their children to do well in school, but they also want them to "have a life outside of school." They bristle at the thought that their children are not being challenged enough in their classrooms, but at the same time they do not want their children to have homework that could challenge them even more. Many of them envision their children as successful adults, both materially and professionally. Naturally, they want their children to lead happy and comfortable lives, and they know full well that this kind of future will not fall out of the sky and into their laps. It is clear to me that teachers are picking up on parents' seemingly contradictory attitudes, and articulating a middle ground that can be even more confusing for children. Many elementary schools have adopted homework policies that are inconsistent with teachers' pedagogical goals:

> Of course we want children to do their homework.
> But the reality is that some children find
> assignments to be relatively straightforward and

complete them in about fifteen minutes, which is
what we recommend. Others need much more time
to understand what it is we are asking them to do,
and much more time in which to do it. So we tell
parents, if the homework isn't done in a 15–25
minute time frame, then tell your child to stop.
They will have done enough, and we will always
take it up again the next day.

              —*Mrs. Jackson, third grade teacher*

Ironically, the message to students is that they have homework to do, but it is really OK if they do not get it done in a certain
amount of time. How might children make sense of this? Some
may be thrilled, and dawdle through their twenty-five minutes,
knowing that's as much time as they need to spend on their work.
Others, though, might come to think that they lack the ability to
do the work in the recommended time. If they cannot accomplish
what others in their class can, they must not be smart enough. Despite their good intentions, then, teachers may very well send an
unfortunate message to children and their parents.

This ambivalence toward academically challenging experiences in general, and homework in particular, is difficult to fathom
in light of the fact that the very parents of whom I speak worked
very hard and sacrificed plenty of opportunities to "goof off" while
they were preparing themselves for the lives they now lead. Many
are grandchildren or great-grandchildren of immigrants, and most
cannot lay claim to large inheritances that will sustain their life-
styles. They would not have gone to the schools they attended, met
the spouses they chose as life partners, been living in the homes in
which they live and the communities in which they have settled
had they not worked very hard to educate themselves. Somehow,
though, many seem determined to shield their children from the
pressures they themselves experienced.

Somewhat ironically, this trend in parents' views about home-work and academic standards flies in the face of generally accepted stereotypes of middle- and low-income parents. Observers of educational trends have written eloquently about middle-class parents who do their maximum to accelerate their children's learning. The popular conception is of parents who are pushing their children at increasingly earlier ages to attain language, literacy, and computational skills that are far beyond what they are ready to learn, and doling out plenty of money to "make it happen." In selected pockets of our society, parents are well aware of which preschools will give their children the best chance at admittance to the best elementary schools, which in turn will maximize their chances of being admitted to the best prep schools, which will open the door to coveted Ivy League colleges. Yet these same parents do not want their children to experience the stress that accompanies homework.

At the same time, given that urban children tend to do worse in school than their suburban peers, it has become commonly accepted that poor and minority parents do not care about their children's education and pay little attention to their development, intellectual or otherwise. But I learned from my work in Boston's public and Catholic schools that although many parents may perceive that they are limited by their own poor education or rudimentary English language skills, they are undeterred in supporting their children's education in a variety of ways, including setting and maintaining high standards for schoolwork and encouraging their children to work with friends in what becomes essentially a study group. Whatever else we may think about living in a society that is still quick to make judgments based on race and social class, parents are well aware that education is still the primary ticket out of poverty. Despite what may have been their own unhappy academic experiences, many poor parents are acutely aware that their children's future ability to support themselves and find job fulfillment lies in the institution of schooling. In short, they are clamoring for the very things middle-income parents are desperate to protect their children against: high standards and more homework.

## Academic Competence: Where Our Children Stand

As I mentioned in Chapter One, the 1980s saw us inundated with distressing facts about the massive underachievement of American children as compared to their Japanese and Chinese peers. In one early study, American and Japanese first graders did not differ very much in their mathematics skills. By fifth grade, however, the achievement gap had widened to the point where the highest-achieving U.S. classroom was doing about as well as the lowest-achieving Japanese classroom. Quite alarmingly, researchers found that the average achievement of the *highest-achieving first-grade Japanese* classroom was equivalent to the *lowest-achieving U.S. fifth-grade* classroom.

By the 1990s, international comparisons expanded to include surveys of mathematics achievement in forty industrialized nations. Here too we found no reason to take pride in our children's accomplishments. The Third International Mathematics and Science Study of seventh and eighth graders found that the mathematics competence of American students is significantly inferior to that of their peers in half of the forty nations sampled, including France, Austria, Japan, and Singapore. In contrast, American students outperformed their peers in only seven participating nations, including South Africa, Colombia, and Romania, countries that have had more than their fair share of civil and economic unrest. As the saying goes, this is nothing to write home about.

Clearly something is amiss. We are a vital and creative nation, and I don't know how we could have let this happen. And let me be clear that all of us—parents, teachers, and principals—have no one but ourselves to blame. None of us is happy about this state of affairs, yet we continue to be overly concerned about our children's self-esteem and their development into "well-rounded" individuals. If we are genuine about wanting our children to have the best chance at a good future, we need to start embracing the very ideas we are so quick to reject: that children need to try hard, sacrifice more pleasant pastimes for their schooling, and endure the normal frustrations and hardships that are a natural part of learning. This is where homework comes in.

## The Pros and Cons of Homework

> I don't mind if my children have homework, as long as it's not stressful.
> —*Frances, mother of fourth and seventh graders*

> I don't mind if my children have homework. I think a reasonable amount of responsibility is appropriate—it's good for them.
> —*Paula, mother of third, fourth, and sixth graders*

Homework has an overall positive influence on academic achievement. In other words, children's academic performance improves as a result of doing homework. Beyond this overall statement lie several complex relationships:

- Homework is beneficial when it focuses on simple tasks that require practice rather than on more complex tasks that involve higher-order skills.
- The greatest benefits are seen at the *high school* level, especially when students do at least five to ten hours of homework per week. Any more time spent on homework has a continued positive influence on learning.
- At the *middle or junior high school* level, achievement is enhanced by an optimal range of five to ten hours per week. Anything more demanding does not result in children learning more.
- Homework in the *later elementary school* years has relatively little effect on academic achievement.

🌀 Homework has no effect whatsoever on academic achievement in the *early elementary school* years.

In addition, it appears that for children of all ages, homework
can undermine their intrinsic desire to learn, make them focus on
grades (the *outcome* of learning) rather than on discovery (the *process* of learning), and lead to an overall disillusionment with schooling. In other words, homework, especially in the younger grades,
can damage children's natural motivation to learn. In light of these
distressing findings, those of us in the educational community have
done what we are so good at doing: we have adopted a very narrow
and shortsighted view of the benefits of homework, much to the
detriment of our children's ability to become resilient in the face of
difficulty or setbacks.

Buoyed by the educational research on homework's limited benefits, many parents have come to believe that children's social and
emotional development is ill served by the stress that homework can
bring for children and their parents. What these well-meaning individuals are overlooking is the fact that the assignment of homework, over time, serves to foster qualities that are critical to learning:
persistence, diligence, and the ability to delay gratification. These
become increasingly necessary features of school success as students graduate to higher levels of scholarship in middle school, high
school, and beyond. We and our children are in for quite a shock if
their first serious encounter with demanding homework occurs at
around middle or junior high school, as is the case with Ricki, whose
son began middle school this year as a sixth grader:

> You cannot believe what Jet has had to do, in social
> studies alone! The kids had to choose an American
> historical figure from the 1800s, and Jet chose Daniel
> Boone. This was no simple term paper. They had to
> read two books on their character, making notes on
> index cards as they went along. Then they had to
> conduct a survey of at least ten people about whether

they thought it was right for Boone to hunt for a living, and code and summarize the answers on a grid.
This was followed by an interview they had to design
and conduct with an adult who was familiar with
Daniel Boone and his contributions to American
history. Finally, they had to include a complete list
of references. The teacher required a rough draft of
each step in this project, and it all culminated with
final drafts of each aspect of the assignment. No
exaggeration, Jet spent three entire weekends working on this project. And I spent three entire weekends helping him stay organized. And this is just one
course out of five that he is taking! When I think
back to fifth grade, the longest assignment he ever
had took a total of three hours.

Notwithstanding what many educators have come to believe
and what many parents would *like* to believe, children need the
years between first and fifth grade to develop all manner of skills
and strategies to help them cope with the demands that teachers
place on them. Over the years, these demands become increasingly
complex, as do the problem-solving strategies that students must
develop in order to meet the teacher's expectations. The fifteen-
minute assignment of first grade gradually stretches into the three-
week assignment of fifth grade. The years in between will be the
training ground for our children's development into (relatively) organized and mature learners. Early experiences with homework
may not contribute to children's *academic* development, but they
certainly promote their *motivational* development.

From my vantage point in the "homework wars," this crucial
issue is all but lost on the players in the debate. Going back to my
comments in Chapter Three, many of us find it quite natural to
assume that the "smartest" children have it all, that their inherited
gift of intelligence will see them through any and all difficult learn-

ing experiences. In fact, as I stated, the ability to do well in school is predicted less by children's IQ scores and more by their motivational qualities, such as their willingness to tackle new and challenging assignments, to be persistent even when setbacks occur, and to trust that effort can enhance their abilities. Given the choice, I would much prefer that my own children be less "smart" and know how to work their way out of an academic jam.

In other words, a homework assignment is much more than a request to put a dozen words in alphabetical order or complete a page of simple computations. For many children, it is their first experience with responsibility and obligation. Even though they may not be able to articulate it as such, they know that the adults in their lives have obligations to them—to house, feed, and care for them. With the onset of homework, they learn that they too have an obligation to their parents and teachers to do what is expected of them. In assigning homework, teachers communicate that they both know and expect that their children can do the work. Children's homework requires them to listen to the teacher's instructions, remember to put their homework in their backpacks, take it out at home, sit down, and complete the work. It also requires them to know how to ask for help when they feel the need. Once they have completed the work, they need to remember to put the work back in their assignment folder to take to school the next day. Multiply this experience over the weeks, months, and years of elementary school, and what you have at the end are children who understand that they are accountable to their teachers and parents for the quality of their learning, despite the myths:

MYTH 1: *Homework robs children of their childhoods.*

> What has happened to the time for just playing?
> Boys and girls no longer have time to climb trees,
> run, or play. Our children are participating more
> and more in highly organized activities . . . these
> programs, in addition to heavy homework, may be

more than a child can handle emotionally. Teachers
and parents together must remember children have
physical, mental, and emotional limitations. When
they participate in dancing lessons, piano lessons,
church affiliated groups, competitive sports, and
religiously complete long homework assignments,
after a full day of growing and learning in school
each day, there may be emotional devastation and
bankruptcy.

—*An educator, 1968*

Although these words were written three decades ago, they ring
true today for many parents and educators. There is indeed something idyllic about the notion that childhood is or should be a care-
free time, unfettered by responsibilities and worries. Clearly, no one
would advocate loading children up with duties beyond their years.
At the same time, daily homework is not such a burden that children fall apart at its mere sight. There is no reason why we cannot
expect a minimal amount of responsible behavior from our children at an early age, and increase their responsibilities reasonably
as they grow. This is how we let our children know that we believe in them and their abilities. In other words, there is a middle
ground: we can both recognize that children should be given the
freedom to grow and express themselves and at the same time expect them to learn that they too are accountable to others—their
parents and teachers. Despite what some educators believe, it is not
a bad thing for children to learn responsibility and know that life
cannot always be fun.

Taking a cold shower teaches discipline too; and,
compared to doing homework until 11 P.M. three or
four nights a week, it would probably do more to
keep kids awake in school. As for learning that life is

demanding, perhaps being in school seven hours a
day is demanding enough.

—*Educational commentary, 1968*

How interesting that when this statement was written, children *were* in school for seven hours a day. Three decades later, the public school day for most children is about five hours long, and overall academic achievement has plummeted. Yet here we are, worried about how much time children spend in school and how much homework they have to do once they get home. Are our children so fragile that they cannot tolerate a fuller school day and homework afterwards? There are a great many children in urban schools, with far fewer advantages, who are excelling in rigorous schools and loving every minute of it. Children can have homework *and* enjoy their childhoods. Our expecting anything less robs them of opportunities to grow into mature learners.

MYTH 2: *Homework undermines children's love of learning.*

No one can deny the joy of learning that we see in young children's faces. During the preschool and kindergarten years, the vast majority of children can't wait to get to school in the morning and enjoy everything about their day. Unfortunately for many children, this intrinsic love of learning gradually wanes, and many come to see school and learning as a burdensome obligation that they no longer enjoy nearly as much as they used to. In short, they aren't having as much fun anymore. For most parents, this is a rather disconcerting development. Children should feel as happy and excited about learning in fifth grade as they do in kindergarten. Or should they?

The intellectual demands placed on fifth graders are much more complex than those placed on kindergartners. Much of what children learn from three to five years of age is physical and social in nature, as we and their teachers focus on developing their gross and fine motor skills as well as their ability to make and maintain friendships. What's not fun about learning how to pump your legs so you can swing higher? What's not fun about making a collage (thus getting those little fingers prepared for writing)? What's not fun about Monday morning circle time, when you get to talk about your weekend (thus learning how to listen, respond, and wait your turn)?

It should come as no surprise to anyone that by the second grade, our children aren't experiencing the same kind of fun anymore; they simply aren't doing the same kinds of things anymore. Teachers now ask that they learn how to follow multiple instructions, perfect their handwriting through practice, learn their multiplication tables. And yes, children are now on the receiving end of evaluations that come in many forms: the teacher's verbal and nonverbal feedback, grades (or checks, check-pluses, and check-minuses), and report cards. Naturally, this heightens their worries about how smart they are, especially in relation to their peers. And so, naturally, it has become very popular to blame our evaluative system of schooling in general, and teachers in particular, for the children's waning interest in learning.

However, this lament over the loss of an intrinsic desire to learn is misplaced. Instead of blaming homework and grading (and by association, teachers), we should focus on how to teach our children to maintain their interest in learning, even when school is not so interesting anymore. *This* is where we stand to gain the greatest payoff for all our efforts. I can pretty much guarantee that as our children progress from elementary school through the high school years they will have to enroll in courses that are exceedingly dull or difficult (or both) for them. They will gradually enter the realm of "not having any choice," the bane of many high schoolers (and adults). The ability to tolerate boredom, difficulty, or utter disinterest is critical to children's development into mature learners. After all, when was the last time *you* experienced a year in which every event in every single day was fun? Why is it that we think our children's daily lives should be like this? Although schooling should not be a drudgery of Dickensian proportions, it does not need to be perpetually fun and exciting either. It is really OK if our children are not happy about school all the time. That's life, and they have to learn to deal with it. They are much better off learning to cope with disappointment and frustration in the relatively safe environment of their elementary schools than years later in their places of work, where no one will tolerate what will then be labeled "bellyaching."

MYTH 3: *Homework intrudes on family and leisure time.*

Half Moon Bay, California, made headlines a few years ago when school board member Garrett Redmond proposed an outright ban on homework. "Homework is burning out students terribly," he said. "It interrupts family life." In some communities, parents forbid their children from doing any homework at all and demand that they not be penalized.

> Natasha Mayers, an artist whose daughter attends seventh grade in the central Maine hamlet of Whitefield, regularly sends notes back to her daughter's teachers saying she stopped her daughter from doing homework. "She'd keep going, but I'd cut her off after three hours," Mayers said. "Otherwise, we'd have no family time—and she'd have no time to read, to draw, to play."

It is not difficult to understand and sympathize with this mother's perspective. Yet there is another way to look at this problem. Her concerns seem to imply that in her home, there is "homework time" and "family time." Why make the distinction? Why can't homework be built into the time that we spend with our children as a family? Listen, for example, to these parents' strategies for dealing with homework:

When my children come home from school, they
have a snack and relax for a while. When I get home
from work, they help me make dinner and set the
table. When we are done with our meal, we clean
up, then sit down at the table again. My husband
and I read the newspaper or go through our mail
while the children do their homework. At some
point, my husband will put a snack on the table.
They know we're right there to help them if they
need us. My fifth grader will sometimes help my
third grader. We've never had any real problem with
this—maybe it's because it's what we've always done.

—Margarita, *mother of two*

For me, the best part of my day is when I sit down
with my son [a second grader] while he does his
homework. People talk a lot about "quality" time,
and I've never been quite sure of what that means.
But I do know that this *is* quality time for us. It's not
all seriousness—we laugh and have a good time, and
I know what's going on with him in school.

—Abel, *single father*

Our approach as parents makes all the difference. If we resent
the amount of homework our children are assigned or the fact that
they are assigned any at all, our children will pick up on our attitude and act on it, and we will all pay the price. To be sure, there
are many times when we find ourselves disagreeing with our teachers and principals about homework, sometimes vehemently so. As
parents, we have to deal with our differences in ways that do not
undermine teachers' ability to teach and children's ability to learn,
an issue I take up in detail in Chapter Five. In the context of our discussion here, however, it is clear to me that we sabotage our own
efforts to instill the importance of education when we complain

openly and bitterly about homework. We cannot expect our children to take school seriously when we are dismissive of the school's means to educate them.

MYTH 4: *Homework increases inequality in education.*

One of the more unusual complaints about homework is that it unfairly penalizes students whose home life is "unstable," who do not have the benefit of the home environment that middle-class children enjoy. This concern over "inequality" is both shameful and disingenuous. It recalls the attitude toward poor families that prevailed in the 1960s, a time when educators believed that something was "wrong" with poor families and that intervention could "fix" their deficiencies. The implication, of course, was that if poor families could be made to resemble or function like white middle-class families, the achievement gap between rich and poor, majority and minority, would cease to exist. With time has come the realization that white middle-class parents are not necessarily exemplars of "good" parenting and that poor and minority families have many strengths that enable them to foster academic achievement under stressful life circumstances.

If we were to take this belief about inequality to its logical conclusion, we would need to stop assigning homework altogether, a rather convenient state of affairs for opponents of homework. No one would win, and everyone would lose. The most damage would be done to poor children, toward whom we would have communicated our unequivocal lack of confidence and low expectations for achievement. These are the very children who need to know that we believe in them and in their abilities. There is every indication that they are as up to the challenge, if not more so, as their middle-class peers.

For example, Boston is home to two experimental "full-service" schools whose purpose is to provide the most challenging and rigorous academic environment possible for poor, inner-city children, most of whom were underachieving or failing in public school. At the Epiphany School in Dorchester, the fifth and sixth graders arrive at seven-thirty in the morning and leave at eight in the evening, eleven months of the year. They eat, study, and play together. They have their three daily meals together, adhere to a dress code, have homework every day, a detention hall, and a study hall from six to eight each evening. As an Episcopal school affiliated with the church, children study the Bible but are enrolled regardless of their faith.

> Still, on the Friday after Thanksgiving, this is where Carole Poyer's two sons wanted to be. "They couldn't wait for Monday," Poyer said. . . . "My kids didn't read novels in public school. Now they are excited about reading a book. It's a major difference."

Bear in mind that these are not the "smartest" children, plucked from their public schools because they are the most likely to succeed. These are children of whom much is expected and to whom much support is given. This school, and many others like it, is the clearest indication we have that children are not doomed to collapse when we are appropriately demanding of them.

## Helping, Hindering, and Knowing the Difference

Many parents are unsure of how to help their children with homework, or whether they should even help at all. Some educators push for parents to completely disentangle themselves from their children's homework, whereas others argue that parents should be there to supervise and check their children's work each evening. Extreme positions such as these rarely give us truly useful advice. The truth is, you are the best judge of what your children need, and it may take you a while to figure out just what your children want from you. Doing so is indeed a tricky business. Personality is what

makes our children unique, so what works for one child may be disastrous for another, as this mother recounts:

> With my older boys, who are three years apart
> [twelve and fifteen years old], I never had any
> concerns about homework. It would be done by the
> time I got home from work. My eight-year-old
> daughter is so different. She waits until I get home to
> start her homework. For some reason, she needs me
> right there next to her. I can't even say that she asks
> for my help very much. She just wants me next to
> her, and when it's done, she always asks me to check
> it over for mistakes. She's just more anxious about
> this than my boys were at the same age. In fact, they
> would have gone nuts if I had hovered over them the
> way my daughter wants me to hover over her.
>
> —*Juanita, mother of three*

No matter what works for you and your children, you also need
to strike the delicate balance between offering too much or too little assistance. Take the lead from your children. When they are
tackling long division for the first time, for example, be there to
provide initial support through explanations and examples. Do a
sample problem or two with them. Then back off just a little, let
them take the reins, and be prepared to step back in when they get
stuck. Provide hints, do another sample problem together, and let
them take over again. Over time, slowly dismantle the scaffold of
assistance I talked about in Chapter Three, so that they reach the
point where they can do the problems unassisted. Above all, let
them struggle with confusion. As painful as it is to see children
labor to solve a problem, it is in the struggle that they will gain a
deeper and deeper understanding of the material.

There is no question, however, that struggle for the sake of
struggle does children no good whatsoever. For example, spending

thirty minutes on one long division problem is counterproductive. Give your children *some* time but not *too much* time to try to solve a problem. The goal is not to prevent your children from having to puzzle through a problem, but rather to avoid having them reach the point where they are so frustrated that they cannot focus on their work. In this sense, it is very helpful to maintain regular contact with your children's teachers, for they can give you rough guidelines for how long a particular assignment should take. With this information in hand, you are better equipped to judge when or under what circumstances you should provide some assistance.

By providing too much help, though, you send the message, intended or not, that you do not think they can do it on their own—that they aren't "smart" enough. How much is too much? Any help, when it comes unsolicited, is too much help. Put yourself in your children's shoes. If you were quietly going about your schoolwork and the teacher stopped by your desk to give you some pointers, what would *you* make of this? You were doing fine, not having any problems, and all of a sudden, there she is, giving you hints for the next problem. As it turns out, many children assume that the teacher thinks they *need* the help; maybe they aren't doing as well as they thought they were. Otherwise, why would she have bothered? The same reasoning applies at home. Be mindful of how and when you step in to offer help. In other words, bite your tongue. Resist the temptation to jump in and make things easier for your children. The last thing you want to do is put your children in a position of questioning their ability; your good intentions can ruin the day.

Doing homework *for* your children is too much help and in fact is more of a hindrance in the long run. It is *their* homework, not yours. When you provide answers or solutions to a given problem, you are robbing your children of many things: the knowledge that comes from having to think through a problem, the realization that effort can compensate for whatever lack of ability they may feel they have, the satisfaction that results from finally figuring something out, and the all-important lesson of responsibility and individual accountability. Where homework is concerned, no child is too young to know that she has an obligation only she can fulfill.

- ◉ Know that different children need different kinds of support.
- ◉ Strike the balance between too much and too little and provide an *appropriate* amount of support.
- ◉ Let your children struggle with confusion.
- ◉ Do not give unsolicited help.
- ◉ *Never* do your children's homework for them.
- ◉ *Never* pity your children for the work they have to do.

## "Did You Do Your Homework?"

What a familiar refrain, and one that is echoed nightly in most homes. Many parents struggle with the enduring dilemma of whether they need to check to make sure their children have done their homework. Many of us differ on philosophical grounds. Some believe that making sure their children have done their homework goes hand in hand with teaching them to be accountable for their actions. In other words, children will not develop into students who will do their homework unquestionably if they are not under the scrutiny of their parents, at least in elementary school, if not beyond:

> There is *no way* I would let Anne [a fifth grader] go
> to school without her homework done and checked
> over. I feel it's very important that she be prepared
> to learn the next day, so I would also never let her go
> to school with mistakes in her math or spelling. I
> don't correct her mistakes—I just point them out
> and have her try to figure out what she has done
> wrong.
>
> —*Ruth, Anne's mother*

Look, I'll be honest with you. Some parents would
find this embarrassing, but Tim is in the eleventh
grade, and if I don't ask him if he has done his
homework, he won't do it. Our friends say we have a
"chicken and egg" problem—that we have always
been like this, so he never learned to take the
responsibility for himself. They may be right; I don't
know. All I know is that we have to do what we
have to do, and at this point, we have to check up
on him. If it's our fault, so be it. He'll be in college
soon enough.

—Leo, *Tim's father*

Others feel very strongly that these lessons of responsibility and
accountability can be learned only if parents back off entirely. Parents may not be happy sending their children off in the morning
knowing that they have not done their homework, but their goal is
to have their children learn from the teacher that there is a price
to pay for ignoring his assignments.

Enough is enough! I'm not going to baby him
anymore. After all, I'm not going to be there in
college checking up on him. I say, let him get in
trouble. Let him learn the hard way—it's the only
way he's going to learn.

—Glenda, *mother of a ninth grader*

This dilemma is tricky precisely because it involves the teacher.
We never know what teachers will think of us as parents if we have
a hands-off philosophy. If our children are not doing their homework, it would not be unreasonable for teachers to think that it is
our fault, that we are uninvolved, or that we simply don't care.
Whether we like it or not, the opinions that teachers form about us

from just such issues can influence how they think about our children. My own parents cared very deeply about how our behavior reflected on them. To go to school with our homework unfinished was unthinkable, not only because they saw it as our "job" but also because it would give the teacher the impression that they did not take our education seriously. In short, they would have been terribly ashamed of us if we did not uphold our end of the "contract," so to speak.

Some people call this narcissism, but I call it guilt. No matter how much I might have hated a teacher or a subject or a particular assignment, I would never have let it go. Others may have thought I was a "goody-two-shoes," but I knew better. I did my homework diligently for three reasons: (1) I had to, (2) my parents would have felt ashamed and disappointed in me if I didn't do it, and (3) the teacher would have been really mad at me if I didn't do it. The irony is not lost on me. Here I am, a student of intrinsic motivation, acknowledging that although I have always loved learning, external concerns played a powerful role in motivating me to do my work and to do it well. In my particular case, being worried about external factors was not such a bad thing.

In Glenda's case, her son continued to "forget" his homework or claim either that he did not have any or that he had done it. Six weeks into the second quarter of the year (sometime in December), Glenda received a letter from his science and math teachers, each of whom advised her that her son had not handed in the ten assignments that had been distributed over the course of the preceding weeks. At a meeting held at the request of the teachers, they let her know how disappointed they were in both her and her son. In the end, Glenda learned the hard way that there are some children who need supervision even throughout high school.

Again, you are the best judge of what works for your children. You must be prepared, however, to be flexible. Glenda learned from other mothers that it had been years since they had had to verify that their children had done their homework. She was very angry at her son and felt quite embarrassed. I let her know that she had no choice but to put her anger behind her and give in to doing what she felt she should not have to do. In short, the stark reality was that her son needed the kind of supervision most others did not.

## How to Handle the Battles

Every evening is a nightmare. There is nothing in the world that Emma hates more than homework. Invariably, she ends up in tears, and we are beside ourselves with frustration. I hate to tell you this, but there are days I dread coming home from work. I just don't know what to do anymore.

—*Dorothea, mother of a fourth grader*

I laid down the law two nights ago. I have had it up to my ears with the hassles over homework, and I can't take it anymore. Between you and me, I think the school's policy is crazy, and I would *never* assign an hour of homework every night to a third grader. That doesn't change the fact that it has to be done. So I told my twins that from now on, they have to do their math homework as soon as they get home. They can relax until after supper, and then they have to sit down to finish whatever reading or writing work they have left to do. To be honest, I think the tone of my voice scared them. But it seems to be working, and as long as it's working, I'm not backing down.

—*Jennifer, mother of a third grader*

It reached a point where we were just batting heads. There is just something about our interaction over homework that isn't working. I've tried every strategy in the book. The more I tried, the more

belligerent he got. So I took myself out of the
equation altogether. I hired a college student who
comes over every day from 4:00 to 6:00 P.M. She
supervises Fred's homework and gives him whatever
help or tutoring he needs. It's finally peaceful at
home again.

—*Elsa, mother of a fifth grader*

Very few of us indeed can attest to having stress-free experiences with homework. Clearly some days may be better than others, but there are times when all children "lose it" over homework. The best way to quell the homework wars is to head them off at the pass.

- Set a pattern for yourself and your children from the very beginning. Plan a routine—any routine—as long as it is a consistent one.
- Select a time that works well for everyone—after school, before dinner, after dinner—it does not matter.
- Have a place to do homework that is comfortable for your children—the kitchen table, their own desk, on the living room floor.
- Be as matter-of-fact and as "mean" as you like—homework has to get done, and no one has a choice about it.
- Prepare yourself for all manner of tantrums; eventually, your children will calm down and accept the bitter pill of responsibility.

Homework is not about intellectual development. It is about motivational development. It is about helping your children become mature learners—students who will see homework as a daily obligation they *have* to fulfill, students who will be able to resist taking time off when they have a lot of work to do, students who will know how to seek and not avoid help when they are struggling. As school gets increasingly difficult and courses become more complex, your children need to be persistent when the going gets tough. Homework, as much as you and they may hate it, will foster these strengths of character.

# CHAPTER 5

# Working with the Teacher's Values

Last year, when Liza was in the third grade, the teacher sent home a list of spelling words that the class would be tested on every Friday. This year, she's had just one spelling test, and it's already November. I'm concerned about this, but I don't know what to do. Should I go to the principal? Should I speak directly to the teacher? It's an awkward situation.

—*Bonnie, mother of a fourth grader*

I can't believe the amount of homework Joe is bringing home every day. It's insane. Last night, which was typical, he had to put the week's spelling words in alphabetical order, write a sentence using each word—there were ten in all—and then draw a picture illustrating each word. That took him about an hour. Then he had two pages of addition and subtraction. That took him about a half hour to do. He was really bushed by the end of it all. As far as I'm concerned, the whole thing is excessive. I made an appointment to see Mr. Sargent [the principal] tomorrow. He's *got* to speak with the teacher.

—*Candace, mother of a second grader*

At some point in their schooling, our children will inevitably be paired with a teacher whose values, teaching style, or discipline practices do not match our vision of what "good" teaching should be like. When we find ourselves, as did Bonnie and Candace, in uncomfortable positions, how do we handle them in a way that won't offend the teacher or alienate us from the principal? And how do we see that our children's needs are met without undermining their respect for their teacher?

Working with your teachers' values requires you to balance your own reasoned judgments with your perceptions of the teacher's goals for his classroom. Despite the fact that this is neither easy nor straightforward, you need to keep in mind a larger view of your children's schooling:

- Reflect on what you really want for your children.
- Be respectful of your children's teachers.
- Never criticize the teacher in front of your children.
- Be there for the teacher, to support her work.
- Get involved in the classroom in any way that your schedule allows.
- Feel free to meet with your children's teachers when you have a concern.
- Advocate for your children when you are worried about how the teacher is treating them.
- Don't sweat the small stuff.

Many of you may think that I am naive, and you may be right. Yet bear with me while I try to sort out this issue, which is a difficult one for me. I view the teaching profession from three perspectives: as a teacher of graduate students, an educational researcher, and a mother of school-age children. I know how hard it is to meet the varied demands of adult learners, some of whom can be irrational and quite capable of adult-sized tantrums. Perhaps this has made me more mindful of the difficult task that teachers of children and adolescents face on a daily basis. As well meaning and caring as a teacher may be, the reality is that he cannot always attend to the needs of each of our precious children at the precise moment the child needs him. Although this may not make me happy, I have learned through my own children's incidents that sometimes being ignored, too, is a learning experience. In other words, my children have to learn that their needs cannot always come first in a classroom with twenty-five other children present.

When I speak to parents about their concerns regarding their children's teachers, I inevitably find myself saying, "Be careful what you wish for." I have had parents complain bitterly about the lack of challenge in their children's schooling yet voice concerns about assignments that are, in their judgment, too complex and stressful. As much as we might like to have it both ways for our children, we can't. And we shouldn't. If you want your children to experience challenging learning opportunities, then know and accept that these opportunities will involve some stress for them. The overall goal is not to ensure a stress-free education for your children but rather to teach and model for your children ways to cope with stress when it rears its ugly head.

## What to Do When You Disagree with the Teacher's Methods

In Chapter Two I talked about how I learned to hold back from correcting kindergartners' spelling mistakes. I accepted the teacher's position that focusing on the children's errors would make them conscious of spelling every word correctly, and would ultimately result in an increased reluctance to write. And so, like some other parents, I learned to live with the new philosophy behind invented spelling. Others, however, were not as sanguine, especially if they had had other children learn to write in this way:

Invented spelling was a disaster in our household! It took several years for my two oldest children to "recover." For that matter, the concept seemed to reek of the whole self-esteem building phenomenon: don't let kids feel bad about their writing; they'll get discouraged. Yes, mistakes are most definitely our friends, but it seemed as though invented spelling involved inviting the mistakes in for tea.

—Beth, *mother of three*

In Beth's mind, her older children had struggled needlessly as a result of a teaching method (or "fad," as she put it) that did more harm than good. Determined to prevent similar problems in her youngest child, she met with the teacher, explained her family's experiences with invented spelling, and told the teacher that she planned to supplement the writing her son did in school with spelling instruction at home. Whether or not the teacher was happy about this, Beth cannot say. However, Beth feels strongly that this strategy worked for her and her son, and she has no regrets.

Beth's approach was an appropriate one, in the sense that she shared her concerns with the teacher, letting the teacher know the context in which her doubts about invented spelling had flourished. She was neither antagonistic nor judgmental toward the teacher, who reiterated the long-term value of invented spelling. Ultimately, the teacher had no real choice other than to accept this one mother's disappointment with a widely accepted method of writing instruction. In this kind of situation,

- Consult with the teacher, and seek his or her advice.
- Know what you are talking about. Be very well informed about the philosophy of instruction you disfavor.
- Be equally informed about the supplemental method of instruction you plan to use at home.

- Be prepared for the possibility that things may not turn out as you planned. For example, you may find that you have confused, rather than helped, your child.
- Be flexible—seek other advice from the teacher and other parents.

## What to Do When the Teacher Is Too Demanding

Alex has never gotten grades like this before. He was a straight-A student before this year. Now it's all he can do to maintain a B-plus average. He is really discouraged. He feels like there's nothing he can do to satisfy Mrs. Smith. It's really painful for me to see this little scholar of mine depressed over his grades. I'm really upset.

—Marjorie, *mother of a sixth grader*

Brittany found out she will have Mrs. Smith next year and had a complete fit. I have to tell you, though, she has never brought home anything under an A. At all the parent-teacher conferences we've heard nothing but fabulous things about Brittany. I know she is a good student, and I know she loves school, but I also know that Brittany, and we, need to have feedback that's useful. We don't need another teacher telling us what a great kid Brittany is. We need a teacher who will give us the good with the bad. I'm glad she has Mrs. Smith—I feel that at least we'll get a more accurate reading of how she is doing and how she can improve.

—Norma, *Marjorie's friend*

Alex and Brittany have a teacher who holds her students to high standards. Having spoken with Mrs. Smith, I know that she is deeply bothered by rampant grade inflation. In her middle school, average grades hover around A-minus. She is determined to make her grades meaningful and has garnered for herself the reputation of a "really hard grader." She is the one teacher no student wants to get.

Mrs. Smith is not alone in her concerns. From primary through graduate school, grade inflation has become the bane of educators. Think of the irony: relative to one and two generations ago, we are granting high and higher grades to students who are less and less competent. Mrs. Smith is determined to buck the trend and has little support among her colleagues and the parents whose children she teaches.

I am not comparing Norma's and Marjorie's reactions for any reason other than to demonstrate that Norma's approach is ultimately far more useful. This does not make Norma a better parent than Marjorie; it simply puts her in a position to be more helpful to both her daughter and Mrs. Smith. Feedback that is consistently glowing is not feedback—it's a compliment. Your children don't need compliments; they need constructive criticism that will give them the tools they need to sort through confusion and learn from mistakes.

At the same time, I do not wish to minimize Marjorie's concerns. It is very distressing to see a previously engaged and enthusiastic learner sink into discouragement because he is earning grades far inferior to what he is used to getting. In a situation like this, you need to help your children see the greater value in receiving feedback that is accurate rather than vacuous:

- Talk with the teacher. Enlist her help, and touch base now and again to update her on how things are going.
- Disengage yourself from your children's grades.
- Focus on strategies for mastering the material.

Emphasize improvements from one assignment to the next, even if there is little or no change in grade.

For the most part, teachers want and need to know how their students' parents are managing learning at home. There is absolutely nothing wrong or inappropriate with sharing your concerns with the teacher. In doing so, you stand to learn more about the reasoning behind her grading and other policies, which can help you help your children through discouraging experiences such as the one I have depicted. In Marjorie's case, she met with Mrs. Smith to air her concerns:

> Alex is so discouraged with his grades. You know what a good student he has always been. Now he thinks he's dumb. He doesn't want to do his homework anymore, and there are days when he doesn't even want to come to school. To be honest, I'm discouraged, too. Can you give me some ideas for helping him—ideas that will make him feel better about all this?

Clearly, Mrs. Smith's goal was not to have her students come to believe they lack the ability necessary to do the work she is assigning. She explained to Marjorie that as a twenty-year veteran of the public school system, she had seen a gradual rise in all children's grades. This kind of grade inflation bothered her, because she is committed to giving children and their parents feedback that is genuinely useful. In other words, Mrs. Smith gave Marjorie a context in which to understand her grading philosophy; she tried to get her to see how her teaching experiences have shaped her beliefs about grading. Mrs. Smith emphasized that she believed that getting an A is no longer an indication of competence in Alex's school and that she is determined to provide students with an academic experience in which a high mark is reflective of mastery. Mrs. Smith was not going to change her grading practices for one student, but she did talk with Marjorie about coping strategies that would work for Alex in particular. In social studies, for example, she encouraged Marjorie to go over her written feedback with Alex and to keep a list of things he should pay attention to from assignment to assignment, such as clear and concise introductions, correct spelling and grammar, and proper use of subheadings.

The difficulty level of assignments is another issue that divides parents:

> Rebecca is only in second grade! Ms. Jones has them doing this really complicated research project. They each have to pick an African American they admire and write a report. She's teaching them to use the encyclopedia and the Web to get information. They have to take notes, keep track of their sources, and write about this individual's history and contributions to American society. I didn't do stuff like that until I was at least in high school or even college. I don't like it—it's too much to ask of children at this age.
>
> —*Alice, mother of a second grader*

> Josh is only in the second grade! I can't believe what Ms. Jones has them doing. They're writing an actual research report. They're using the encyclopedia and the Web to gather information, taking notes, doing a lot of writing, and in the end, the whole thing is going to be sent out to be professionally bound. It's fabulous—I didn't do this kind of stuff until at least high school or maybe even college! And the greatest thing is that Josh, totally on his own, is reading lots of other books about Colin Powell.
>
> —*Bette, Alice's friend*

I believe very strongly that we do our children a terrible disservice when we are reluctant to have them take on challenging projects, such as the one described by Bette and Alice. We need to have more faith in teachers' sense of what our children are capable of learning. Many teachers, especially those who have been members of the profession for twenty or more years, are witness to the overall decline in expectations for children's performance in school. Recognizing the level of underachievement in the nation, many are determined to spark their children's enthusiasm through creative and challenging projects. We parents need to support teachers' attempts to infuse their curricula with assignments and projects that stretch our children's minds.

- Embrace challenge, so that your children may do the same.
- Do not fear hard work, for you might influence your children to approach projects with trepidation.
- Ask the teacher how you can support your children as they work to complete a complex project.

## What to Do When the Teacher Is Too Easy

The pace is as slow as molasses. Listen, I'm not saying Evan is a genius, but he is bored to tears. It's kids like him who suffer when the teacher has to teach to the lowest common denominator.

—*Linda, mother of a third grader*

Now that Melanie has finished fifth grade and is starting middle school in September, I'm reflecting more and more on her elementary school years. I know this is going to sound crazy, but Melanie basically drew her way through elementary school.

—*Joanna, mother of an entering sixth grader*

For every family who worries that schooling is too stressful, there is a family who worries that it is effortless. When you find yourself in this situation, your best option is to supplement your children's learning. I don't mean to imply that you should give them more homework on top of what the teacher assigns, but rather that you can engage your children in conversations, activities, and events that reinforce and push their thinking and reasoning skills forward.

One excellent option open to some of you is a mixed-age classroom, such as a combined kindergarten and first-grade class, or a second- and third-grade class. Not surprisingly, there is debate over whether the younger or older students are getting the "better end of the deal." In fact, both groups benefit in very different and challenging ways. Parents know that much younger children really look up to older students. As occasional "teachers," older students are peers, not adults, and that difference makes the process of learning seem less judgmental. For their part, parents of older students are generally worried that their children's learning will be jeopardized by the presence of children who are, on average, a full year younger than theirs are. The truth is that mixed-age classrooms offer unique opportunities to both younger and older children. Those parents who suspect that their older children will end up "doing the teacher's work" really have nothing to fear. As those of us who are teachers know, we deepen our understanding of a topic when we are asked to teach it to someone else. The same principle applies to children on an individual basis. If your child enjoys the company of a younger child now and again, encourage them to spend time together; perhaps your child could work as a "mother's helper" or, if he or she is old enough (say, ten to twelve years of age), as a tutor to a younger student who needs help. I know from my own experiences that getting together as a family with other families provides all the children with opportunities to play with older and younger kids. Of course, the same-age friends largely stick together, but we find that all the children really enjoy spending some time as a large group.

You can also involve your children in community activities.

Most children, by seven or eight years of age, enjoy feeling that their contributions can make a difference. Involvement in community work expands children's scope of the world in which they live and gives them deeper perspectives on their lives and the lives of those around them. A growing sense of political and social awareness leads to wonderfully rich dinner conversations, which give you and your partner opportunities to encourage higher-order thinking.

Some parents and teachers do not view enrichment programs as a positive addition to their children's learning experiences. Organizations such as Score@Kaplan and Kumon Math have sprung up in recent years, presumably to fill some parents' needs to give their children a jump start as early as possible over everyone else's children. I was well aware of this stereotype, and when one of these organizations opened a storefront in our community, I avoided it like the plague. The overall philosophy of the organization is rooted in extrinsic rewards for learning, something I find difficult to reconcile with my desire that my children learn for the sake of learning. At this establishment, children learn through computer-assisted instruction and receive tokens for meeting certain prescribed goals. They can then exchange these tokens for prizes, which are handsomely displayed in a glass-fronted cabinet for everyone to see.

I had studied the educational research on extrinsic learning, and the whole notion rubbed me the wrong way. All indications are that rewards for learning undermine children's intrinsic interest in all things academic. Nonetheless, the fateful day arrived when my daughter was taken there by a friend, who was a member (you get tokens for bringing in a friend, too). Well, she was beside herself when she came home. As far as she was concerned, it was the most incredible place in the world, and she just *had* to become a member. The very idea of refusing to let her go to a place where she seemed to enjoy learning was bizarre, so a year later and $99 per month poorer, I can honestly say that it is indeed a wonderful experience for her. I have had the chance to witness the work that young college graduates—the "coaches"—do with the children, and the children's learning extends well beyond the tokens and prizes. What really matters to my daughter and many other children who attend are the *relationships* they form with the coaches, who take an enthusiastic interest in each child. I believe that my daughter would continue to attend even if the tokens were eliminated. She loves the coaches, she loves what she is learning, and she loves to see her progress on summary reports that we receive every three months. These are quite an incentive for her. So I say to those who, like me, would be quick to criticize enrichment centers: I learned that the influence of extrinsic motivation in actual experience can be quite different from that described in the textbooks.

It is important to note, though, that the decision to enroll my daughter was hers, and hers alone. We did not suggest, cajole, or force her to join. I cannot be sure, but this *must* make a difference in how she perceives the whole experience. I suspect that when children are forced to join an enrichment center, their experiences may not be as positive. When parents make the decision to sign their children up, they are implicitly saying that they think their children need the help. As I have said in earlier chapters, this kind of message can cause children to doubt their abilities and undermine their confidence. Therefore, be mindful of how your children might interpret a membership in an academic enrichment center.

- Encourage get-togethers with a mixed-age group of children.
- If your children are old enough, encourage them to tutor younger children who need help.
- Involve your children in community activities, such as food drives.
- Visit a nearby academic enrichment center—the first visit and session are usually offered free of charge.
- Let the decision to join an enrichment center be your children's.

## What to Do with Social Problems in the Classroom

> I'm telling you, there are three kids in the classroom
> that need to be peeled from the ceiling on a regular
> basis. They are unbelievably disruptive. It's a wonder
> anyone is learning anything. How can the principal
> let this happen? I'm making %#!&! sure Emily is not
> with those kids next year.
>
> —*Ray, father of a first grader*

As much as we would love for our children to be in a classroom
that matches our vision of what a learning environment should
look like, these matters are largely out of our control. Unbeknownst
to Ray, the principal does not allow parents to make peer requests
for class placements, except under extreme circumstances, such as
bullying. This kind of policy offends many parents, and they hold
a defensible position, to a point. After all, why should everyone's
learning suffer at the hands of two or three children who, for whatever reason, are out of control? It's unfair, plain and simple.

When my daughter was in kindergarten, her coat hook was
next to a boy who thought it was funny to jump on her head whenever they had to get their jackets. I said the usual things we are
taught to say when our children are in preschool. "Tell him it bothers you and ask him to stop." No luck. "Tell him he can't do that to
you because it hurts." Nothing. Irritated, I finally told her to mention it to the teacher. "What did he say?" I asked the next day. "He
told me to duck," she replied.

I was so taken aback—I had expected that he would punish the
boy somehow, perhaps banish him and his coat hook to the other
end of the hall. But then I thought, this is great. Instead of making
a punitive fuss over the incident, the teacher gave my daughter a
strategy, a way to think about getting out of a situation that made
her uncomfortable. In many ways, this is the "second curriculum"

*Is this the best way to deal w/ student conflicts?*

of schools. Your children need to know that there will always be other kids who will be pains in the neck, and they have to learn how to cope in problematic social situations. And as much as we would like not to admit it, our children will inevitably be someone else's pain in the neck; some other child will have to learn to cope with our disruptive bundle of joy. And so, as much as I would like my children to be placed in ideal classrooms with ideal children, learning from an ideal teacher, this is not going to happen.

And now that my daughter survived the "boy-jumping-on-her-head" incident (which of course, she did indeed survive), I have come to see that very valuable learning of a social and psychological nature occurs in classrooms that we would not necessarily hold up as exemplars of ideal learning environments.

- ✇ Be attentive to your children's complaints about other children, yet learn to take everything with a grain of salt.
- ✇ Value the important life lessons, good or bad, to which your children are exposed.
- ✇ Except under extreme circumstances, avoid orchestrating the "best" classroom for your children.
- ✇ Help your children learn to cope with peers who are causing them distress.

## When to Advocate and When to Back Off

I know that it takes longer for Jimmy to catch on to concepts in his algebra class, but that's no reason for him to be in Regular Algebra. He'll be much better off in Honors Algebra; so he'll have to work harder, big deal. The important thing is that it'll look a heck of a lot better on his transcript.

—*Danielle, mother of a ninth grader*

His teacher told me to keep Lewis in the Regular
track, at least for social studies. His writing needs a
lot of work, and she said he'll just sink in Honors, as
much as I would like it. We talked for a long time,
and in the end we agreed to set a goal for this year
that would have him in Honors next year. We have
a lot of work ahead of us. . . .

　　　　　　　　　　　*—Lynn, mother of a ninth grader*

As immigrants to a strange land, my parents could afford the luxury
of believing that our teachers were operating with our best interests
at heart. The open anti-Semitism they experienced in the workplace was not evident in the public schools, and my mother and
father never had any reason to doubt our teachers' assessments, the
good and the bad. Unfortunately, a great many parents today have
reason to consider it a folly to accept every evaluation at face value.

The sad reality is that as the population of minority children living in poverty grew, it became increasingly apparent that many of
them were being treated unfairly in public schools. For example,
educational researchers find again and again that poor African
American and Latino children are vastly overrepresented in low-
ability groups in elementary and high schools across the nation. Put
another way, poor and minority children continue to be consistently
placed in lower-ability tracks in numbers disproportionate to their
representation in the population. By definition, then, these children
are vastly *underrepresented* in high-ability groups and college prepara-
tory tracks. Their parents need to do their maximum to ensure a
quality education for them. There are indeed times when we have
legitimate concerns that we must address, and we need to feel
empowered enough to speak out and advocate for our children.

Every school has a mission statement that spells out its goals
for the children's education. This statement is usually found in the
parent handbook, a valuable tool for all of us. Familiarize yourself

with your school's policies, especially those dealing with discipline. Different schools have different ways of dealing with academic and social problems. Knowing what these are before an incident occurs gives you a leg up on how to work in partnership with the school to improve your children's performance or behavior (or both).

At the same time, awareness of school policies allows you to detect instances of unfair treatment and the mechanisms for redress. A hot-headed verbal attack on your child's teacher or the principal is unlikely to yield your desired result. No matter its size, a school is a bureaucracy, and we parents have no choice but to "go by the book" when we have a legitimate complaint.

Official school policies may make no mention of ability grouping or tracking, yet most schools engage in some kind of separation of students on the basis of test scores or classroom grades. Familiarize yourself with *if* and *how* this practice is carried out in your school, and be aware of where your children are being placed. Group and track placements are an integral part of children's evaluative "paper trail," and as your children get older, the direct consequences of their placements for their later education loom large. Our system of education is set up in such a way that by middle school many children are already tracked into courses of study that will dictate whether and where they can go on to college.

For example, it is critical for students to take a prescribed sequence of mathematics that leads to the study of calculus, for calculus is a requirement for college admissions. If your children find themselves in a course such as Business Math, they will miss altogether the opportunity to take Algebra I and II. At that point they will probably never be able to take calculus, because they will have not fulfilled the algebra requirements. Having never taken calculus, they will find their college options greatly limited. In other words, your children's education gets set on a trajectory early on in their schooling, a trajectory from which relatively few students can veer.

Clearly, not every child is gifted, exceptional, or in a position to be placed in the highest groups or tracks. This is not a bad thing. Do not advocate for higher placements for the sake of having your children in the "best" group, for that group may be the *worst* placement for them. In their zeal to ensure the best possible education, many parents inappropriately pressure principals and teachers to have their children follow a particular course of study for which their children may not yet be prepared. And teachers get an earful from the students themselves, who resent the pressure their parents are exerting on them. Many students are happy to learn in Regular rather than Advanced Placement (AP) or Honors courses or prefer an AP course in the one subject they enjoy the most. The undue pressure you would place on your children in situations like this could very well backfire. Indeed, the last thing you want to do is set your children up for unnecessary failure.

By all means, be vigilant about the academic experiences to which your children are exposed. At the same time, however, have some faith that your children's teachers know what they are talking about. You will be in a better position to judge the value of their evaluations if you stay connected to teachers, in whatever ways you can. The better they get to know you and your family, the better you get to know them. Where your children's academic and social development is concerned, this is a win-win situation. In an era when so many mothers and fathers work outside the home, educators are increasingly sensitive to the need to reach out to parents. For example, this year my children's elementary school introduced the "Back and Forth Book," a blue-lined notebook in which we and the teacher could write notes to one another, asking questions, seeking clarification, or communicating a concern. Teachers checked and responded to the notebooks daily, and this proved to be a source of comfort for many parents.

In this context, it is regrettable that in many middle-class communities, parents have taken their activism to extremes, feeling entitled to complain about any and all aspects of school policy in general, and teaching practices in particular. In an era when parent involvement in the classroom is mightily encouraged, there exist entire school systems that forbid parents from volunteering in their children's classrooms. Many principals note with sadness that parents see these volunteering assignments as opportunities to spy on their children's teachers and report back what they consider to be unacceptable behavior. The entire endeavor, once so valued as a way to assist teachers and build a sense of community, has crumbled under the weight of unreasonably demanding parents.

This development is partly fueled by misinformed perceptions of teachers as individuals who are not very smart and who entered into the profession not for their love of children and teaching but for lack of anything better to do. It is no secret that the teaching profession in this nation garners little respect. Relatively low salaries and a general failure to attract the brightest college students have given some more educated and wealthier parents license to assume that they know better than the teacher what to teach and how to teach. Such parents as these feel and act on a misguided sense of entitlement. It is rather commonplace to question policies, from the hiring of faculty to the delivery of school lunches, and to offer unsolicited advice to teachers and principals at the drop of a hat. I have no doubt that this overall demeanor sends a clear message to children that their parents think it is OK to question anything and everything that happens in the classroom. Many teachers have lamented the amount of time they spend answering the Why questions: Why are we doing this? Why do we *have* to do this?

I am saddened by the extent to which it has become increasingly popular to blame teachers for everything that is wrong with our educational system. For example, the fact that our students are doing so poorly, especially in math and science, cannot possibly be the sole fault of teachers. They do not work in a vacuum; they struggle in a larger system that needs to support and not undermine their efforts to do their jobs as best they can. By all means, be vigilant throughout your children's school years, but temper your attentiveness with the knowledge that you need to know your place.

- ◈ Avail yourself of your school's handbook for parents.
- ◈ Familiarize yourself with your school's ability grouping or tracking policies.

- Stay connected to your children's teachers.
- Know what your children are doing in school.
- Do not let nagging concerns drag—address them immediately.
- Seek redress when you believe your children are being treated unfairly, yet have some faith that the principal and teachers know what they are doing.

## Show Respect for Your Children's Teachers

She's an idiot. She expects the kids to do their homework *and* a preparation sheet for the next day, supposedly so they'll be familiar with what she's going to teach. It's way too much. Jeremy knows he has to do his homework, but as for this coo-coo preparation thing, I told him to ignore it altogether.

—*Janet, Jeremy's mother*

If you ask me, the whole preparation sheet idea is ridiculous, and you can't imagine the fits at home. Once Angie has finished with her homework, it's like pulling teeth to get her to complete the preparation sheet. She says it's not like "real" homework, and she doesn't have to do it. Then she tells me that other kids aren't doing it because they think it's stupid, too. Well, at that point I had no other choice but to launch into my "Every-house-has-different-rules" speech and let her know she has no choice. She has to do it because the teacher assigns it—end of story.

—*Daniel, Angie's father*

You must show your children that you respect their teachers as individuals and as educators, *especially* if you do not feel this way. You cannot possibly expect your children to take school seriously if you make them privy to your disdain and dislike for the teacher. The beliefs you share with your children invariably influence the beliefs they form about their teachers. Even if the teacher is "bad" in your judgment, you will inflict more harm than good if you commiserate with your children about their teacher's terrible qualities. In the short term you may make them feel better by confirming their views, but in the long run you will undermine the teacher's authority in the classroom, her ability to teach, and by extension your children's ability to learn. Your explicit condemnation of the teacher's negative qualities gives your children license to scorn her attempts to teach them. The damage extends well beyond your children's experiences with this one teacher. They will come to think that they can wield power that is not theirs to wield, a belief held by too many students already.

There are other, appropriate ways to express your dissatisfaction with your child's teacher. Bonnie, whose dilemma with her daughter's teacher opened this chapter, decided to address the inattention to spelling by writing a short letter to the teacher. The letter was cordial and simple. She expressed her concerns and asked the teacher if it might be possible to spend more time on spelling. The teacher responded (also by letter) in a way that left Bonnie unsatisfied. Undeterred, she wrote to the principal, who thanked her for her input and scheduled a meeting with all the fourth-grade teachers to discuss how spelling is handled at this grade level.

> When I was in fourth grade, there was a girl named
> Karen who was an unbelievable bully. For some
> reason, she chose another girl, Missy, to pick on; she
> really tortured her. I happened to know Missy pretty
> well because she lived a few doors down from me.
> She was *really* shy—I guess today she would have

been labeled "pathologically inhibited" or something. Anyway, one day, Karen just went too far. She was passing around a note that said Missy's mother dresses her like a baby, and of course the note made it into Missy's hands. At recess, Missy was crying, and Karen came over and starting taunting her. Well, I don't know what happened, but something inside me snapped, and I pushed Karen to the ground and punched her in the stomach. Needless to say, the teachers were on top of us in a split second. I got suspended for a week and sent home immediately. My mother, who was expecting my arrival, met me at the door with a look I'll never forget. I walked in and started to tell her the whole story of the injustice (in my mind), and she cut me off. As far as she was concerned, I was *way* out of line, Missy was not *her* concern, and she *never* wanted me to behave like that again. She made me write an apology to my teacher, the principal, and *Karen!* Talk about humiliation. . . . Later, when she calmed down, she told me the most important thing to her and my Dad was that we respect the teachers and the school.

—*Jackie, twenty-six*

Somehow, I cannot see many parents today reacting the way Jackie's parents did some sixteen years ago. I think many parents would be proud of Jackie's actions and commend her for having come to the aid of a weaker student. Yet the lesson of respect that her mother tried to instill in Jackie still clings to her, and in retrospect she is grateful to her mother for having opened her eyes to another, deeper perspective on the relationship between children and their teachers. Jackie's mother's way may not be your way, but the lesson is there nonetheless.

◉ Respect your children's teacher in word and in deed.

◉ Orient your children to the teacher's perspective and goals for the classroom.

◉ Handle disagreements discreetly.

# CHAPTER 6

# Balancing Extra-Curricular Interests with Academic Obligations

As far as I can tell, everyone has gone mad enrolling their kids in so-called enrichment centers and getting them tutors for this, that, and the other. Everybody wants their kids to get straight A's so they can get into the best private school that will give their kids the best chances to get into an Ivy League college. Enough already! School isn't the only thing in my children's lives, nor do I think it should be. I'm sorry, but kids have to have a life outside of school. I don't mean to offend, but I don't want my kids to be geeks, know what I mean?

*—Dan, father of a fifth and eighth grader*

As far as I can tell, everyone has gone mad enrolling their kids in a million different after-school activities. I have to tell you, the pressure is on to have your kids do all this fabulous stuff outside of school. We agreed to let Annie enroll in three activities—soccer, ceramics, and gymnastics— and I really resent it now. I don't want to be in competition with other families for who is doing the

---

This chapter was coauthored with Norma V. Jimenez.

> best activities in the best centers in Boston. We're
> exhausted, and I'll admit that Annie is happy, but
> she's tired. So—brace yourself—we did the
> unthinkable—we took her out of everything when
> she started having fits over being too tired to do her
> homework. She hates us for now, but who cares,
> know what I mean?
>
> *—Joe, father of a sixth grader*

Both of these fathers have taken a good look around them, and both believe that the other has gone mad. I listen to the both of them and can't help but feel that we are all going mad, in one way or another. Balancing academics and extra-curricular activities has become a very, very difficult and delicate task for many parents. The issue is a very emotional one, and one that divides parents on philosophical grounds.

It is only natural that we would wish to expose our children to different sports, arts, music, and the like. After all, it is through early exposure that children discover for themselves the passions they will carry into adulthood. It is not healthy for any child to be focused on only one thing, whether it be schoolwork, soccer, or the violin.

And as your children grow, it is only natural that their interests become more varied and their attentions increasingly divided between schoolwork, extra-curricular activities, and, for many, part-time jobs. Most parents are delighted to encourage interest and involvement in activities outside of school. Many see participation in athletics and the arts as providing opportunities for tremendous social and psychological growth, especially where children's self-esteem is concerned. Many also encourage their teenagers to get part-time jobs after school as a way to teach them the value of money. Inevitably, though, conflicts arise that pit school achievement against out-of-school activities, or even out-of-school activities against one another. For too many parents, these conflicts are compounded when they allow their *own* self-esteem to get tied up in their children's extra-curricular accomplishments, creating problems not foreseen when their little boy started Suzuki violin lessons or when their little girl kicked the soccer ball around for the first time.

The conflicts become even more complex when your children are in high school. The college admissions process has become increasingly competitive, and "simply" being an exemplary student is no longer enough to ensure admission into our best institutions of higher learning. The coveted spots and scholarships are not won by the excellent students; those go to the "well-rounded" students. In their attempts to sort their way through whatever pressures they perceive society to be impinging on them, many parents, like Dan and Joe, have embraced extreme positions, which will ultimately backfire in one way or another. It doesn't have to be this way. Like Dan and Joe, we all need to find a balance between our children's academic obligations and their development in other areas.

## Less Is More

Social, economic, and political changes in postmodern society have inarguably altered the fabric of contemporary family life, and many parents cope with the multiple stressors of jobs in the workforce, households to maintain, and children to raise. For a great many families, this complex system is managed without the benefit of nearby extended family members, who a generation or two ago could always be counted on in a pinch to care for a sick child, greet the school bus in the afternoon, or bring dinner over. The two-parent family with a stay-at-home parent today accounts for less than 10 percent of all two-parent families. At the same time, with the current rate of divorce and single parenthood, it is estimated that more than half of all children from birth to eighteen years of age spend several years (or their entire childhoods) living in a single-parent household. Many more children are being cared for outside their homes: in day care, in after-school programs, and, with concerns about safety at the forefront, at organized sports activities.

Never has the expression *less is more* been more meaningful than in the debate over extra-curricular activities. Too many suburban parents are succumbing to the frenzy that has become organized sports and are driving themselves and their children into the ground. Sally, a suburban Boston mother, recounted to the *Boston Globe* a typical afternoon with her three children:

> 3:15 P.M.: Baseball practice for Michael, 9, at Warrandale Park. Michael is dropped off with the coach because:
>
> 3:30 P.M.: Mary, 10, has Girl Scouts at the Cedar Hill Girl Scouts camp. Sally is the den mother.
>
> 4:30 P.M.: Girl Scouts is over, so it's back to Warrandale to pick up Michael.
>
> 5:00 P.M.: Christopher, 7, has a make-up soccer game at the field on Trapelo Road.
>
> 5:30 P.M.: Forget about Mary's baseball game at Warrandale; no one can be everywhere at once.
>
> 6:00 P.M.: Christopher's soccer game ends; drive Mary to soccer practice at the Army Corps of Engineers field. Whoops: it's not practice; it's a rescheduled game. Drive back home, grab uniform, and drive back.
>
> 6:30 P.M.: Fortunately, the game starts late, so Mary makes it just in time.
>
> 7:30 P.M.: Home, for a supper of sandwiches.

I find Sally's commitment to her children's development admirable, but at the same time I wonder: How exhausted are Sally and her children when they get home? Is there energy for lively discussion about the day's events over their sandwiches? Because they have been in and out of the car since 3:15 P.M., no one has done their homework. Given the afternoon's events and the relatively late hour, how will "homework time" go? Will the children have any time with their father? Will Sally have time alone with her husband? When will everyone get to sleep? Of course, it doesn't sound as though anyone is unhappy or suffering. But what has become of their family time? And what is behind this craziness?

## The "Ideal" Child

> When you live in an area like this [Ridgefield, Connecticut] you get caught up in it. If you don't do each step, you feel like you're doing an injustice to your kid.
>
> —*Janice, mother of a fourth grader*

We have a collective and cultural notion of an "ego-ideal" for our children. Broadly speaking, North American society embraces a view of the ideal child as one who is skilled in many domains. Although education is certainly a top priority in most families, we tend to view learning as but one aspect of healthy psychosocial development. We do not tend to value children (or parents, for that matter) who place high value on intellectual pursuits. Rather, we laud the student who is popular, athletic, musical, and artistic and is also a good (but not necessarily excellent) student—this is the "well-rounded" student of whom I have been speaking.

In all my years in school, as a student, a teacher, and an educational researcher, I have never met anyone who fits this description. This is probably why we conceptualize such a person as an "ideal" student: he or she exists only in our imaginations. Yet when push comes to shove, it is not the superlative student we value the most but this ephemeral vision of the "student for all seasons." Not surprisingly, this idealized vision gets us and our children into a lot of trouble and is the cause of unnecessary family conflict.

In many cases, when conflicts between children's school and extra-curricular obligations arise, many parents feel reluctant either to diminish involvement or to remove their children altogether from outside activities. Some, like Dan, fear that their children will turn into "geeks," "nerds," "brainiacs," or other derogatory labels we have to describe exemplary students. Other parents worry about precious time lost in the development of pitching (in baseball) or slap shot (in hockey) techniques. Still others feel that any commitment made is a commitment to be honored—they work hard to teach their children that they have a responsibility to themselves and their teammates or band partners or whatever—a responsibility that cannot be taken lightly. Do these parents mean to imply that their children's academic obligations can be taken lightly? I doubt it, but I suspect that this is the underlying message that their children hear.

> Even in the most intense programs, children will tell you what they want: the sheer fun of the game, the tribal bond with teammates, the pride of being selected for a team, *and the attention from busy parents who might not make as much of a fuss over a triumph in algebra or Spanish* [emphasis added].

And of course, many parents worry that removing their children from an activity that brings them so much pleasure will undermine that supposedly delicate aspect of everyone's personality: their self-esteem.

## The False Promise of Self-Esteem

> We've led a lot of people astray about self-esteem—children feel good about themselves when they can read and write.
>
> —*Deanna Burney, educator*

We have become a nation obsessed with the belief that self-esteem is everything—that a lot of it predicts the best life outcomes and not enough of it dooms children to lifelong despair. In other words, children must be made to feel good about themselves, for those with high self-esteem are the only ones headed for happy, healthy, and fulfilling personal and professional lives. The self-esteem "movement," such as it is, has far surpassed its characterization as a bandwagon on which parents and educators have clamored to board—it has become a runaway train with no one at the controls, and it is proving to be our academic undoing. We have managed to collectively fabricate beliefs about children's self-esteem that are patently false: that children's self-esteem is terribly fragile, that their development into well-adjusted adults is built on the foundation of self-esteem, that children need to have *a lot* of self-esteem to sustain them through difficult experiences and transitions in life, and that any indication of low self-esteem puts children at risk for a variety of social and psychological problems, such as alcohol and drug abuse, teen pregnancy, and delinquency. In truth,

- Self-esteem is not a thing or an entity—it is a quality that changes over a lifetime.
- Self-esteem cannot be given—it must be genuinely earned.
- Self-esteem is neither high nor low—it unfolds along a continuum from low to high.
- Self-esteem cannot be perpetually high—it is always in transition; thus it's OK for your children to have low self-esteem, especially considering that self-esteem varies with different components of the self.

I am certainly not *against* children feeling good about themselves. I *am* against the extent to which raising children's self-esteem has become a goal pursued at the expense of academic enrichment. Many teachers, concerned about the multiple stressors to which so many of their students are exposed, wish to be able to ease their burden. Regrettably, a great many children find themselves mired in predicaments not of their own making, such as messy divorces and custody battles. Their struggles are heartbreaking, and it is very difficult to stand by and observe those struggles every day. And so teachers' good and well-intentioned objectives are often realized by lowering standards. It is not uncommon for many schools to eliminate or reduce homework loads and to assign tests and homework that are easy enough to ensure success. In addition, through social promotion, the practice of promoting failing students for social reasons, unprepared students are advanced to the next grades so as to avoid the embarrassment of being left behind.

This collective effort to shield children from disappointment or failure is a misguided goal that will certainly backfire. As I mentioned in Chapter Four, disappointment and failure provide children with opportunities to learn how to develop coping strategies in the face of difficulty. By protecting (or overprotecting) our children from these experiences, we rob them of the chances to build a repertoire of beliefs and skills that can be truly helpful and that will, ironically, bolster their self-esteem and make them more competent individuals.

## What to Do When School Takes a Backseat

> Basketball is the *one* thing Jimmy looks forward to all week. He was never good in all the other sports he tried—football, soccer, hockey, you name it. And on top of all this, he never had a whole lot of friends. Now he's found something he has a lot of talent for, and he feels great that his coach and the others on the team need him to win—they rely on him a lot. He's got friendships now that will last a long time. Basketball is the only place he gets his self-esteem—how can I take that away? I just can't do that to him—he'll fall apart.
>
> —*Lucia, mother of a tenth grader*

Lucia and her husband came to me with a very serious problem. Jimmy was faltering badly in school, in a variety of ways. His performance was inconsistent in every single subject—he would do really well on one assignment and fail the next. Or worse, he would complete the next assignment but forget to turn it in, and then get a failing grade. Given my personal beliefs, I advised them to pull him out of basketball, at least until he got a firmer grip on his academic responsibilities.

As you can tell from Lucia's comments, she was loath even to think about pulling Jimmy off the basketball team, and with good reason. Surely, they argued, such a drastic measure need not be the first line of defense, and in this I had to agree. My background led me to endorse my parents' all-or-nothing approach to problems such as these, and I had to admit that there was wisdom in seeing if a compromise solution could be found. So Lucia and her husband began generating ideas for how to get Jimmy back on track academically while still preserving basketball in his life. Here is what they did: (1) spoke with Jimmy often and at length about the critical importance of doing well in school, (2) enlisted the help of the coach, (3) worked out a study and homework plan with each of his teachers, and (4) sought regular counsel from the guidance counselors.

Jimmy's parents did their best to get him to see farther into the future than his basketball "career" in high school. Both are well educated, and they knew that a strong athletic background combined with a poor-to-mediocre academic transcript would get him nowhere fast. And Jimmy is a typical "good kid." He listened, he agreed, he apologized, he did a little better, did a little worse, did a lot worse—after some time, his parents' heart-to-hearts turned into battles of epic proportions. Talking, it seemed, had run its course.

The basketball coach had many talks with Jimmy. Together they spoke of his future plans. When Jimmy revealed that he really wanted to play varsity basketball, his coach told him in no uncertain terms that he had to "shape up" academically if he was to have any chance of getting into a decent college with a decent basketball program. These pep talks too seemed to be of limited use.

Jimmy's teachers coordinated a "sign-off" homework book. They each regularly inscribed homework assignments along with their due dates, as well as the dates of tests and quizzes. His parents signed the assignment sheets when they read them, and now had a way to monitor Jimmy's work and make sure he stayed on track with his classmates. Jimmy's guidance counselor was similarly on top of his family's situation. She arranged a meeting between Jimmy, his parents, and the guidance staff, during which they discussed goals and strategies for staying abreast of his schoolwork. All of this was to no avail.

Anger and resentment grew in their household as Jimmy's schoolwork continued to suffer. Although I never met the coach, I doubt that the coach threatened to yank Jimmy from the team if he didn't shape up academically; the team needed Jimmy to win. The sign-off plan went the way of the dinosaurs. It worked for about one month, until Jimmy started forgetting to bring the sign-off notebook home. The teachers lost patience and basically gave up. The guidance counselors empathized with the parents' dilemma but advised them of the dangers of removing Jimmy from the team. They recounted stories of parents who, confronted with a similar conflict, eliminated extra-curricular activities from their children's schedules only to find themselves mired in problems of serious rebelliousness and plummeting self-esteem. With their collective years of service to the high school, they *must* have been witness to success stories, but they chose not to share these with Lucia and her husband.

This drama lasted the duration of Jimmy's four years in high school. Despite all the evidence, his parents never cut back on his basketball commitments—they even allowed him to miss school on several occasions to attend tournaments out of state. Jimmy graduated from high school a mediocre student and has held part-time jobs while he goes to night school to get the grades he should have gotten in high school so that he can get into college. Having had time to reflect on this period in Jimmy's life, I am left with the distinct impression that many parents and educators believe that students' self-esteem either *cannot* or *should not* come from their academic accomplishments. Tongue in cheek, I always tell my students that my mother, given the choice, probably would have preferred I have *no* self-esteem but remain a good student.

In some ways, this is how Jaleh dealt with her daughter's declining school grades:

> When Farnarz started ninth grade, the social stuff went way, way up in all the girls' minds. Who talked to who, who sat where with who in the cafeteria, all of the normal preoccupations of early adolescence. The thing is, she was spending hours on the phone at night. At this point, I expected her to be responsible for her schoolwork. So I made a passing comment one day about all the time on the phone, and she assured me that it was not interfering with her studying or with getting her work done.
>
> Well, the first-quarter report card came back, and she got two C's and a B-minus. I flipped. My husband and I immediately took away her phone privileges, forbade her from getting together with friends during the week, and yanked her off the soccer team. We told her she could only talk on the phone Friday and Saturday nights and could make weekend plans only if her homework was done and checked by Friday evening. She went ballistic, and her friends thought we were two-headed monsters. It took them about six weeks to stop calling the house during the week. Each time the phone was for her, we would patiently remind them that "Farnarz is not allowed to talk on the phone on school nights."
>
> By the third quarter, Farnarz was doing great. She was getting her usual A's and B's, and we slowly eased the telephone back into her life. We also let her play softball. Believe me, she doesn't doubt for

one second that if her grades slip, we *will* take serious action. And you know what? She feels *really* good about herself.

There is no question that it hurt Jaleh and her husband to see Farnarz unhappy, constantly mad at them, and generally miserable to live with for a good stretch of time. They put up with it, though. They had faith that if they hung on to their convictions, Farnarz would see that no amount of pouting, crying, or raving would move them. They never caved in, although they were sorely tempted to on many occasions.

I cannot say with any certainty that this approach would have worked with Jimmy. All I know is that out of concern for his short-term self-esteem, his parents unwittingly set him up for a serious long-term bout of low self-esteem once he graduated from high school. It has been very painful for him to be left behind, watching his friends go off to college while he flounders, trying to make up for lost time.

## Preventing Problems Before They Get out of Hand

Unfortunately for all of us, we cannot have it both ways: there is no way that schooling can take the front seat if our children are over-committed to outside activities. Lest you think that I am a paragon of reason where my own children are concerned, let me share my second grader's schedule from school last year: ceramics on Tuesdays (1:30 P.M. to 2:45 P.M.), Italian on Wednesdays (3:15 P.M. to 4:15 P.M.), Brownies every other Thursday (3:15 P.M. to 5:00 P.M.), soccer on Saturdays in fall, swimming on Saturdays in spring, and Hebrew school every Sunday (11:00 A.M. to 1:00 P.M.).

As a full-time working mother, I was driven mad by the car pooling and scheduling. This year, however, everything will change when Hebrew school becomes more time consuming. My daughter will be going to Hebrew school Tuesdays and Thursdays from 4:00 P.M. to

6:00 P.M. Although the timing would still work out, ceramics will be out of the question. As much as my daughter loved doing ceramics and felt very good about what she made for our home, she will have to give it up, and we will hear no end of it for some time, I'm sure, especially considering that others of her friends in the same position will continue with the course.

This process is replayed over and over in the lives of many families during their children's years in school. The best we can do is sort out solutions to conflicts that work for our individual children and our own families. There is no one formula for sorting out competing demands that can work for all families. In this context,

- Know your limits.
- Establish a list of priorities, and make schoolwork the top priority in your home.
- Communicate your priorities *clearly* to your children.
- Treat extra-curricular activities as *privileges*, not entitlements.
- Maintain your commitment to family rituals, such as eating dinner together.

My bias in this discussion is crystal clear. There is only room for one at the top—one priority, that is. You cannot dedicate the same level of commitment to your children's music lessons or sports practices as you would to their schooling. If from the beginning you relegate outside activities to the level of *privilege*, your children will know and expect that their participation is contingent on their consistent dedication to their schoolwork. And, to paraphrase the quotation cited earlier, by all means *make as much of a fuss over a triumph in algebra or Spanish as a triumph in soccer or ceramics*.

## Coping with the Realities of Getting into College

Do you think for one minute that this is what I had
in mind for Diego? I would like nothing more than
to see him come home after school, relax, do his

homework, and shoot hoops out by the garage.
Getting ready for college is like a full-time job for
him. He is constantly on the go because he *has* to be.
The college recruiters all tell us the same thing:
make sure you have a high GPA, take all Honors-
level courses, get all the tutoring you need to push
your SAT over 1450, do at least one varsity sport
each year, get yourself into a leadership position in
your community, land the lead in the school plays,
and don't forget that volunteer work looks great on
your application. Do all this, but make sure you are
unique in at least one way, because colleges look for
original talent. Sometimes I think we're all pawns in
somebody's big game. It shouldn't be this way; this is
just nuts.

—*Ernesto, father of an eleventh grader*

None of us is parenting in a vacuum. We are all well aware of how
intensely expensive and competitive higher education has become.
The pressure that Ernesto feels is real. The economy is not what it
used to be. A high school diploma is not the armor it used to be.
My father-in-law, who is eighty-two years of age, left school in the
eighth grade to help support his family. As an adult, he was able
to secure a middle-class lifestyle for himself and his family by working as a sheet metal worker in an era when blue-collar jobs were
plentiful, and unions protected your job for life. Today our economy's needs have changed, and job stability is a thing of the past.
A young adult needs at least a college diploma in order to secure a
reasonable job at a reasonable salary. Scholarships are fewer and
farther between, and thus the pressure is on our children to demonstrate to admissions committees that they are the best thing
since sliced bread. Ernesto is right—getting into college and receiving coveted scholarships have become two of the biggest guessing
games—or second-guessing games—in town. As I mentioned ear-

lier, the days when the best-prepared student was practically guaranteed a space on campus are long gone. Nowadays, the "best" students academically are not necessarily the ones winning coveted spots at top colleges.

> At Brookline High, what we see more and more is
> that it [admission to top colleges] makes good
> parents crazy, and that finds its way down to the
> kids, making good kids crazy. . . . The kids have been
> so overscheduled and over-programmed that by the
> time they get to high school, they feel guilty if they
> aren't using every minute productively.
>
> —*Guidance counselor*

The problem is not so much that the rules of the game have changed but that they have become so terribly uncertain. Many students feel they have no choice but to jump on the treadmill, never getting off until the acceptance letter or letters arrive. Sixteen- to eighteen-hour days packed with Honors courses, athletics, community work, part-time jobs, and homework are not unusual, as these students attest:

> Stress, stress, stress. Every night I would go home
> and cry. . . . I'm just waiting for the year to be over.
> Right now, I know I'm graduating, and that's all
> I know.
>
> —*Lisa, twelfth grader*

> You realize even then [as early as freshman year] that
> what courses you take and how well you do will have
> an effect on college. Then, in your junior year,
> everyone keeps reminding you how important
> junior year is.
>
> —*Abbey, twelfth grader*

I feel like if I get one C, I blew it.

—*Rachel, twelfth grader*

To be sure, there are parents who will have prepared their children for this kind of high school experience from an early age:

> You can hire consultants to work with your four-year-old [to get into the "right" preschool]. They'll show him how to maintain eye contact with the interviewer, how to exhibit sharing and cooperation skills in group play. By the time we get to see an application, there has often been a great deal invested. Kids have personal trainers now, individual tutors in every subject. Some parents hire college consultants while their child is in middle school. There's a whole industry now that helps kids prepare applications.
>
> —*Bill Fitzsimmons, dean of admissions,*
> *Harvard College*

Others, though, find themselves horrified at the whirlwind that has become the college admissions process. Ironically, many of these are the same parents who overscheduled their children in elementary school. As you can see from the quotations cited earlier, the scene is not as pretty in high school.

In our anxiety to provide our children with the best education possible, we are led to believe that admittance to an exclusive college will open all doors and provide our children with the best opportunities for further education and fulfilling and lucrative careers. I cannot deny the advantages that come with an Ivy League degree. Yet I know two things to be true. First, such a degree, in and of itself, is not an automatic guarantee of lifelong success and happiness. As the saying goes, life is what one makes of it, and a Yale degree will do nothing for someone who cannot work with others, who is afraid of challenge and responsibility, or who never wanted it in the first place.

Second, life's opportunities are not open exclusively to those who attain degrees from coveted institutions. We tend to forget this in the hype over the competitiveness that characterizes these schools. I pursued my graduate education and now teach at Harvard, but I would never have been admitted to Harvard College to pursue my bachelor of arts degree. My SAT scores were too low, and I was involved in only one outside activity throughout my high school years. This has not held me back, nor did it hold back the many graduate students I came to know in Harvard's dorms, all of whom had graduated from all manner of state schools and second-, third-, or fourth-tier colleges.

A non–Ivy League education does not necessarily hamper students' ability to get ahead. Economist Robert J. Samuelson described a study in which economists compared the SAT scores and later career earnings of freshmen from thirty-four colleges, some elite, some not. Earnings were similar, regardless of whether students had attended an Ivy League school. The reason?

> Characteristics important for admission may also be rewarded in the labor market. What might these be? Discipline. Imagination. Ambition. Perseverance. Maturity. What students bring to college matters more than what colleges bring to students.

It is very difficult indeed for parents to deal with the pressures brought on by the college admissions ordeal. Your best bet in helping your teenagers through this period is to keep a positive and realistic outlook on the entire process. For teenagers, choosing prospective colleges presents issues similar to those that arise when selecting among a list of classroom projects. In Chapter Two, I talked about how you can help your children learn to choose projects or assignments that are neither too easy nor too difficult. In many respects, your task is similar at this stage in your adolescents' lives. Of course, you must convey reasonably high expectations for their post-secondary education. Your beliefs about the next step in their schooling will have a profound influence on their own beliefs.

At the same time, you need to temper your expectations with a healthy dose of realism. One piece of advice that applies to virtually all students is for them to avoid "putting all their eggs in one basket." For example, applying only to the top five Ivy League colleges is not a realistic strategy for any student. At the same time, a student who is fairly academically successful should *not* think that first-tier colleges are beyond his or her reach. In other words, applying to one or two top colleges among a range of different colleges is not unreasonable.

> In my senior year in high school, I had no idea that I could apply to UCLA or Berkeley. I was graduating from a small high school, and I had really good grades. But we were all pretty much encouraged to go to the local college, a small liberal arts college very few people have heard of. My parents just didn't know about other options, and everyone assumed that no one from our high school could get in to a top state school.
>
> —*Tameka, recent Ph.D. graduate*

What if your teenager has a relatively poor academic record? In this case, you need to explore the options that could support her academic development. There exist two-year community colleges, small private colleges, and four-year colleges that will admit students who struggled academically in high school and that offer

varying amounts of support, including tutoring. These different pos-
sibilities mean that it is critical to attend college admissions fairs,
meet admissions personnel, read pamphlets and catalogues very
closely, and *ask, ask, ask* as many questions as you need in order to
ensure a supportive environment for your student. The most important characteristic to look for in a school is that it is a good *match*
with your teenager. You need to have a realistic assessment of your
student's academic needs and social preferences (for example, a large
versus small campus) in order to make an informed choice among
the possible options.

Although the cost of a college education is a serious concern
for many families, cost alone should not deter you from having
your student apply to the range of colleges he has chosen. There are
a great many scholarships, tuition-reduction plans, low-interest
loans, and work-study programs that colleges make available to
their students.

- Be realistic—make a realistic assessment of your student's academic needs and social concerns.
- Don't leave the entire process up to your student; consider it a
  joint venture.
- Inform yourselves: request catalogues; visit prospective
  schools—in person, if you can, or on the Web (on-line); talk
  to current students, ideally ones who fit the profile of your student (in terms of social class, ethnicity, interests); talk to
  alumni or others who may have connections to the colleges
  your teenager is considering.
- After acceptances are received and your student finds herself
  with some choices, take your time as a family to make the
  decision. Reassess the colleges, as your student may have
  changed his mind about his preferences.
- Some colleges have sleepovers. Encourage your teenager to
  take advantage of the opportunity to experience a day or two
  as a student in the life of the college.

◉ Make a list of the pros and cons of the schools your student applied to, and reevaluate these lists after acceptances come in.

## The Dangerous Lure of Athletic Scholarships

> There is no correlation whatsoever between success in youth sports and success at the high school level, and even less correlation with college. In fact, it's just the opposite. I often see more burnout in those kids, an inability to handle all the other parts of being a Division 1 athlete like enthusiasm, handling diversity, getting along with teammates. They have no idea how to do those things because they're being pushed too young into being the best, being a star.
>
> —*Kathy Delaney-Smith,*
> *Harvard women's basketball coach*

For some parents, the motivation to push children into sports comes from the elusive promise of an athletic scholarship to college. The astronomical costs of a college education lead many parents to read more than they ought into their eight-year-old's slap shot. Too many parents place too much faith in their children's early athletic ability. Yet as Delaney-Smith notes, early talent, such as it is recognizable, is not predictive of later talent. And athletic scholarships are ever dwindling, a reality that many parents either are unaware of or prefer to ignore.

Regrettably, their hopes are often raised unrealistically by college recruiters, who now scout out talent when children are as young as middle school age. Those parents who hope to take their children's balance beam routine to the bank are often advised to have their children specialize in one sport very early in order to maximize their talent and skill development. Emphasis is also placed on participation in more competitive teams, such as travel teams, for which children are chosen on the basis of open competitions. It has become the norm for children to play for two or three leagues in their chosen sport. The result is that overuse injuries and reinjuries, previously reserved for the professional athlete, have found their way to children in elementary school, more and more of whom acknowledge the need to play even when they are injured.

A broader perspective on the relationship between athletics and academics is all but lost. I don't believe that this is what anyone had in mind when the world of organized sports opened up. Ironically, it is the children themselves, especially those who have been pushed relentlessly, who find their own kind of balance as teenagers, when a great many drop out of sports altogether—a sad ending to what should have been a childhood spent fostering a lifelong commitment to exercise.

- By all means, foster your children's interest in sports.
- Assume that no athletic scholarship is in their future.
- Encourage your children to find balance in their lives.

## Keeping Your Own Ego in Check

Who among us believes for one second that he is not always thinking in terms of what is in his children's best interest? As I have said before, one parent's actions in the service of her children's "best interest" is another's meddling interference. One thing is certain: as difficult as it may be, all of us need to look deep within ourselves to question our own motivations:

- Reflect on what it is you want for your children.
- Distinguish between what *you* want for them and what *they* want for themselves.

◉ Recognize when you are living your unfulfilled dreams through your children.

◉ Be open to criticism about your children *and* yourself.

There is no doubt that our own egos get wrapped up in our children's accomplishments and disappointments. Admission to a private school or top-level college is, to some degree, a feather in our parenting cap. The competition we may feel with other parents is bound to find its way down to our children, and with no positive consequences. Our children are under enough pressure—even too much pressure—and do not deserve to have our personal concerns heaped on to their own.

The same holds for their participation and performance in extra-curricular activities. Maintain the proper balance within your home and don't be concerned about everyone else. At the end of the day, psychologically healthy children are not the ones who have been pushed to exhaustion in one area or another, but rather the ones who have been encouraged to think about their future place in the world and how they will be able to get where they want to be.

# CHAPTER 7

# Confronting Negative Peer Pressure

Proud Parent of an Honor Student

—*Bumper sticker*

My Kid Beat Up Your Honor Student

—*Bumper sticker*

The particular culture of teens has always been of interest to educational researchers and a source of some concern to parents and teachers. In the aftermath of the student massacre at Columbine High School in Littleton, Colorado, interest and concern have given way to fear, disbelief, and recrimination. The sheer magnitude of the violence directed at students who were members of certain cliques has refocused everyone's attention on the microcosm of society that is the high school.

To be sure, teenagers are no different from adults. They sort themselves or are sorted into groups in much the same way we sort ourselves or are sorted by others. In the workplace, we distinguish between employees and employers, blue-collar and white-collar workers, nonprofessionals and professionals, nonskilled and skilled laborers, the working poor and the poor, welfare and nonwelfare families. These labels carry with them well-defined and often unwarranted stereotypes of what these different kinds of individuals are like, how they live, and what they value. These stereotypes do not emerge out of the blue; they come from us, right out of our mouths and into the ears of our children. Where academic achievement is concerned, the bumper stickers quoted at the opening of the chapter speak volumes about our society's views of exemplary students. They are the "nerds" and "geeks" of teen culture.

Past a certain point, you cannot choose your children's friends for them. Rather than fear the antiacademic messages they will hear or the negative influence of their peers (bearing in mind that your teenager may very well be some other parent's nightmare), arm your teenagers with information that will come to have more and more meaning for them as they progress through their high school years:

- Orient your children toward the future; what they value now may not be what they value later.
- Discuss the different pathways for success in their lives; in other words, speak with your children about their goals and how they can reach them.
- Share stories of how success in school has led to fulfillment and prosperity in the lives of people you know.
- Share stories of how school failure has led to disillusion and disappointment in the lives of people you know.

## The Antiachievement Ethic

In the movie *Broadcast News*, Albert Brooks plays a producer for an evening news show. In a flashback to his high school years, we see his valedictorian address, in which he reflects on the fact that he is graduating just two months before his fifteenth birthday. He suggests to the audience of parents, teachers, and peers that if he had not been so ostracized for being an excellent student, he might not have been in such a hurry to get out of high school.

As the saying goes, in every jest there is some truth. Brooks's amusing take on the experiences of a high achiever demonstrates that we are a society that holds a fundamental and collective grudge against intellectual achievement. The message is everywhere—it's OK to be smart, but not too smart. When President Clinton was elected to his first term in office, several of my colleagues at Harvard's Graduate School of Education, as well as a good number of professors from around the university, spent time in Washington helping the new administration assemble the large workforce needed by virtually every department of government. Many in the media had a field day questioning the ability of Harvard "eggheads" to understand what the "real world" was like. The implications were anti-intellectual at their core.

For reasons beyond understanding, being a scholar, a lifelong student of public policy, had become something to be mocked. Never mind that the very individuals who helped get the new administration up and running work in the trenches every day: in day-care centers, Head Start programs, public schools, homeless shelters, housing programs, and drug prevention and rehabilitation programs. The entrenched stereotype of the Harvard professor—out of touch, in the Ivory Tower, buried in theory—took precedence.

This antiachievement ethic reflects some combination of jealousy, defensiveness, and self-protection, perhaps born of a fear that we might not measure up intellectually when compared with others. Even though we are moving toward understanding that intelligence has many components, most of us still define it in intellectual terms; although we are increasingly aware that children possess musical intelligence, kinesthetic intelligence, and interpersonal intelligence, most of us still understand intelligence be to *intellectual* in nature. Smart people are not the ones who have highly tuned social skills; they are the ones who have *a lot* of mental intelligence and can therefore solve complex problems quickly and easily, or so many of us think. What's more, as I mentioned in Chapter Three, we are a society that believes that intelligence is pretty stable. We simply can't get more of it if we were born with just a little of it— compared to others, that is.

And from Massachusetts to California, the culture that supports antiachievement has paved the way for a growing antiwork ethic. Contrary to common stereotypes, the antiachievement ethic is not limited to poor and minority students:

> At nearly all-white Taft Union High, near Bakersfield [California], the anti-work ethic seems widespread. Many students don't do their homework, so teachers often don't bother giving it. It's a vicious cycle, and one that makes Taft teachers throw up their hands in defeat. "If you assign them to read a story and two-thirds haven't read it, where are you?" [the] English teacher asks with resignation.

## The High School Scene

> They [most students] think we're better than everyone else. But we're not the ones who think that.
>
> —*Honor student bound for college*

The attitude against academic achievement echoes the premium we place on well-roundedness, of which I have spoken in earlier chapters. Teenagers are not blind to the contempt some adults hold toward high academic achievement. It should come as no surprise, then, that students will develop negative views and attitudes toward exemplary students. This wholesale lack of respect for academic excellence could not come at a worse time in teenagers' lives. The pressure to fit into the school culture's definition of "cool" can be overwhelming for some teenagers.

We all know adolescence as a time when students want desperately to fit in, to belong, and to be valued for who they are. It is a period in life when they are trying to define themselves and to separate from their parents. Their search for their own identity, which for many people spans decades, is confusing and sometimes painful. Regrettably, many teenagers find themselves being defined by their school's culture, which, like society at large, finds a box, a label, a pigeonhole for everyone. Student groups or cliques are clearly delineated:

> Jocks (Athletes), Preppies (The popular students who wear designer clothing), Gates (Students in the gifted and talented programs), Techies (Computer geeks enamored of all things electronic), High post girls (Students who like to date only older, wealthy boys), Goths (Fascinated with death, they wear black clothes and paint their nails dark), Skaters (Skateboarders).

Notice that this list contains three designations that describe high-achieving students (Preppies, Gates, and Techies). When these names are added to the other labels I have mentioned elsewhere, the list becomes a little long. I am reminded of studies on cultural influences in language development. Anyone who has taken an introductory psychology course has learned how the Eskimo have more than thirty words to describe snow, a phenomenon that reflects the extent to which these people need fine distinctions to survive their environment. Apparently, members of our own culture feel the need to make increasingly fine distinctions between high-achieving students.

> Why is it that we as geeks, freaks, nerds, dorks, [and] dweebs have to suffer while the clueless, bow-headed testosterone-poisoned "normal" people are allowed to get away with murder?
> —*High school graduate of the class of 1984*

The irony, of course, is that no one individual can ever be defined by a sole characteristic. Yet the labels of teen culture imply mutual exclusivity: if you belong to one group, you can't possibly belong to another. You can't possibly be a jock if you are a techie. In other words, you can't be both athletic *and* smart. You can't possibly be a Gates (referring, of course, to Bill Gates) if you are a Preppie, especially if you're a girl. In other words, you can't possibly be smart *and* popular. Despite the fact that many high achievers are also skilled athletes, musicians, and artists, the labels persist. These stark divisions only exacerbate the effects of stereotyping.

To be sure, there are many students, perhaps those with a stronger sense of self and of their futures, to whom these kinds of labels carry no weight whatsoever. However, for those unsure of their place in the high school scene, the social consequences of being labeled (or of labeling themselves) are not lost on them. From the friends they choose and the peers they exclude, to the clothes they wear and those they would not be caught dead in, to the music they listen to and the music they shun, cliques exist and influence the high school scene and your teenagers' daily lives.

In this context, it does not take long for any student to discern who is and is not valued in his or her school community. In far too many high schools, the best athletes receive great admiration from fellow students and, regrettably, special privileges from teachers and administrators. They are members of an elite group sometimes referred to as the "jock-ocracy." In his book *Friday Night Lights*, Bissinger chronicled one Texas community's fervent commitment to football. Members of the team were excused from doing homework and other assignments, allowed to take non-college-credit courses for credit, and enjoyed the benefits accrued from successful fundraising, including chartered plane trips to "away" games.

The message to students who value learning couldn't be clearer. If you want to do well in school, keep it to yourself. You don't have to be a great student—a good student will do. Don't draw attention to your academic ambitions, but rather be everything to everyone—be well-rounded. Ignore these messages, and you risk being ridiculed by your peers. To be sure, this cultural attitude about schooling and scholars takes its toll on those who value their education, but even worse, it provides a backpack full of excuses for those who are unwilling or unprepared, either academically or emotionally, to work and learn. The excuses, whatever they may be, serve them well, but for a very short period in their lives. The short-term gain in peer acceptance is terribly outweighed by the long-term loss of motivation and goal directedness.

It is no secret that the well-educated and technologically competent go on to good colleges, after which many will land well-paying entry-level positions with room for personal and professional growth. The irony is that the best among them, such as Microsoft cofounder Paul Allen, are slowly emerging as owners of or large stakeholders in major-league professional sports teams.

> Within a few years, "nerd" won't even be an insult, but a term of respect and accomplishment. It will become clear even to teenagers that you can get farther ahead by study and learning than by dribbling, throwing, or skating. Of course, it is unlikely that teen culture will change so dramatically "within a few years." Yet there may be some truth to a new twist on the old adage: the geeks will inherit the earth.

## Give Your Girls the Strength to Be Smart

> We had a family reunion of sorts two weeks ago. I was catching up with one of my favorite aunts, who I hardly get to see. I told her I'd be graduating next year with my doctorate in East Asian languages and literature and that I had already been contacted by two colleges about teaching jobs. She was genuinely thrilled for me. Then she wanted to introduce me to a guy she had brought to our reunion—the son of a

good friend of hers. It wasn't what I expected, but hey, I said OK. Her next words blew me away. Before introducing me to this guy, she said, "Listen, you know how proud I am of you, but please, don't talk too much about your Ph.D. and UCLA and all that. I know I don't have to tell you this. You know what I'm talking about. Men really don't like girls who are smarter than them, so just, you know, just don't talk about it." I didn't know *what* to say, so I thanked her for the advice.

—*Raquel, twenty-five*

Smart girls suffer the indignity of the double whammy—they are "female nerds." Their commitment to academic excellence violates two cultures: the culture of underachievement and the culture of feminine identity. For as much progress as has been made by the women's movement in changing admissions and corporate hiring and promotion policies, we still refer to science, engineering, and technology as "nontraditional" career paths for women. Indeed, young women are vastly underrepresented in the college majors that lead to the careers of the future. The gender stereotypes persist: if a girl is pretty, she cannot possibly be smart. If a girl is smart, boys will perceive her as a threat to their self-worth, as Raquel's aunt was quick to caution her. A smart girl will not be attractive to boys, except perhaps to the "nerdy" boys, who are relatively low on the high school food chain.

Math and science careers, unlike medicine and law, are still considered the purview of the nerds. Although it's acceptable for a boy, there's tremendous peer pressure on girls not to be nerdy.

—*Shauna Sowell, vice president,*
*Texas Instruments*

As I mentioned in Chapter Three, the perplexing problem of gender differences in achievement and self-perceptions of ability has puzzled educators for some time. Although girls outperform boys in all subjects in elementary school, their confidence and expectations for academic success are lower than those of boys. By middle and high school, differences in math and science achievement are minimal to nonexistent, yet the discrepancies in confidence and self-perceptions of ability remain. Unfortunately, instead of tackling the issue head-on, too many educators have sought refuge in proposals that claim to build self-esteem rather than strengthen academic achievement.

In the early 1990s the American Association of University Women (AAUW) released a study that claimed to show that gender bias in the classroom is rampant. Among other things, the study found evidence that teachers call on boys more often than girls. It also found that teachers are quicker to help girls than boys when confusion arises. In other words, teachers were found to be more likely to let boys struggle through a difficult math problem. The result for girls was lower self-esteem and a gradual spurning of higher-level math and science courses. Furthermore, the gender gap in math and science concentration leads naturally to fewer and fewer women in the technological pipeline.

The rising concern over peer pressure and differential treatment in the classroom gave rise to increased interest in single-sex education and sex-segregated math and science classes within coed schools. Many educators believe that, unfettered with worries over what the boys in the classroom will or will not think, girls will feel free to learn, get confused, and ask questions in a classroom or even a school devoid of boys. The claim is that self-esteem will rise and, along with it, math and science achievement.

Yet the AAUW found itself backtracking on its claims when a 1998 report found that girls' achievement in math and science is no better in single-sex schools than in coeducational ones. This more recent study concluded that high expectations and standards for performance, combined with smaller class size and masterful teaching, are stronger indicators of higher achievement than en-rollment in a single-sex school. If we are serious about addressing gender inequities in education, we need to pay more attention to our entrenched attitudes about technological ability, which con-tinue to be biased in favor of boys.

We need to disabuse ourselves of the stereotype that techno-logically challenging careers are unsuitable for girls. And we need to do this early in girls' lives. As discussed in Chapter Two, you need to emphasize that disciplined effort makes all the difference in achievement, whether or not your girls think they are smart. You need to work consistently with them to teach and model for them how to cope with difficulty and setbacks. They need to realize that confusion is an unavoidable aspect of learning. This is especially true in the fields of math and science, where we as a society have come to believe that only those who are innately talented can be successful. In this context,

- ◉ Acknowledge that technological material is difficult but that your children can master it with sustained effort.
- ◉ Teach your children the value of asking for help.
- ◉ Discourage their shying away from advanced math and science just because the courses are advanced.
- ◉ Don't give the message that you did not have the ability to do math and science.

There is no question that these tips apply equally to boys and girls, and should be communicated clearly to both. Know that everyone's self-esteem rises as a result of increased academic com-petence.

## Listen and Share

It is critical for you to hear and understand your teens' concerns. It is terribly easy for us, decades after our own experiences, to advise our children to ignore those who would mock them for doing well in school. After all, most of us believe we survived, more or less intact, and that our teens will also survive. Yet for children at thirteen, fourteen, fifteen, or sixteen years of age, being accepted among their peers is one of the most important things in their young lives.

Regrettably, we tend to rally around our teenagers only when a crisis presents itself. Superintendents and principals appropriately call on social workers and counselors when a school experiences the sudden death of a student, be it through accident, suicide, or, as recent tragedies have shown us, murder. Outside the realm of tragedy, we may not pay as much attention to what is going on in our teenagers' lives. Yet it is in the everyday happenings of "normal" high school life that you stand to learn the most about your teenagers' concerns and worries. As many parents will tell you, some teens talk through their problems (or at least some of them) with their parents; many others are reticent to share.

It is therefore terribly important for you to get to know your teenagers' teachers and the school's administrators. The more you know about the workings of the school and its culture, the better equipped you are to deal with difficulties when they arise. You give yourself the gift of context when you forge connections between the high school and your family. In other words, you are better able to understand your teenagers' problems when you are familiar with the atmosphere and surroundings in which your children spend the better part of their days. Furthermore, you will feel less at a loss for what to do when you know who the players are—the individuals in the school to whom you can turn for advice.

- Get to know the high school and its teachers and principal.
- Pay close attention to your teenagers' concerns.
- Do not minimize your children's worries—they are very real to them.
- Discuss these concerns with friends who have similar-aged students.

It is equally important to share—share your own high school stories, your best friends' stories, good and bad—with your children. Even though they may carry on as though they don't need you, your children do indeed need you desperately and find comfort and sometimes surprise in what you reveal about yourself:

> When I was in the eighth grade, I had kind of had it with rules. My father was unbelievably strict, and he sent us to a school that was almost like a military academy, but not really. Anyhow, I fooled around a lot, nothing too serious by today's standards. One day, though, I crossed the line. This kid who was always in my face just got to me, and I punched him out. I got kicked out of school. My parents told me I now had to find a job and start working. That's why I have only an eighth-grade education, and why I do what I do for a living. I don't want the same for you.
>
> —Misha, father of a tenth-grade boy

> When I was in the ninth grade, I decided to drop out of school. It seemed funny at the time that my parents didn't say anything one way or another. I started working as a house painter with my Dad. The work was tough, and it was always hot and humid. One day, I was up on a ladder next to my Dad, and he asked me to go down to the truck to get him a tool he needed. I headed back when I found the tool, and as I started up the ladder, I swear I saw my life pass before me. Right then and there, I knew I didn't want to be doing this for the rest of my life. I mean, I was only fifteen years old, and this was not the kind of future I had in mind for myself. I finished out the rest of the school year working with my Dad, and then I repeated ninth grade and just continued my education. Funny, my parents didn't say anything

about that either, but now that I look back on that
year, I think they knew exactly what they were
doing by staying quiet, know what I mean?
　　　　*—Naim, father of eighth- and tenth-grade boys*

These are two of many stories that Misha and Naim and their wives came to share with their children. In sharing these experiences, they revealed aspects of themselves that were not exactly laudatory. Yet this is why the stories had such appeal to their children; they got a chance to see that their parents, as teenagers, had done some "bad" things, too—they were not perfect! Your own stories are valuable teaching tools, quite different from those I have discussed in previous chapters but no less profound.

## Orient Your Children Toward the Future

Earlier in this chapter, I talked about Albert Brooks's character in the movie *Broadcast News*. After delivering his valedictorian address, he gets beaten up, cap and gown and all, by three of his classmates. In expressing what he believes to be the ultimate insult, Brooks's character exemplifies what educational researchers refer to as "future time perspective." He screams at his peers that they will never in their lives make more than $19,000 a year. In other words, he has a vision of what his life will look like down the road, and knows that it will be very much better than that of his low-achieving tormentors, to whom a yearly income of $19,000 may as well be a CEO's salary. Indeed, rather than being offended, the bullies are delighted at the thought of making that much money.

On the many occasions when I am asked to speak to parent groups, I am struck by how strong parents' desire is to ensure that their children are happy all the time. This desire keeps many parents from talking about how difficult life can be at times. Be they working parents or stay-at-home parents, I don't know anyone who has had an easy go of it. Of course, from an objective perspective, the life of a parent who does not work outside the home can seem like heaven to those who have to get themselves and their children out of the house every day by 7:45 A.M. and are not back at home until 6:00 P.M. And many parents who do not work outside the home come to envy those who are in one place all day focused on one thing—their jobs (or so they think). They are not the ones in and out of their cars all day long, picking up, dropping off, and doing all the things that working parents hire others to do or do themselves on the weekends. The grass is always greener on the other side, as they say, but believe me when I say that no one's life is a picnic.

Share these kinds of difficulties with your children. In no way am I suggesting that you make your children privy to all your personal problems. Doing so would be irresponsible and inappropriate. It is not improper, however, for your children to know what your day-to-day life is like, what you do for a living, what it takes for you to do your job well, and what it takes in the way of effort to maintain your family's lifestyle, no matter what it may be. I am not proposing that you bemoan your existence in front of your children, or at all, for that matter. I am arguing that *appropriate* doses of reality at *appropriate* times in your children's lives will go a long way in getting them to see further into the future; to realize, for example, that $19,000 a year may seem like a lot of money when you are eighteen years old and still living with your parents but is actually close to nothing when you are on your own or with a family to support.

It is largely because of my own experiences, and those of my friends and graduate students whose parents were also immigrants, that I have come to believe that many children who are oblivious to their parents' hardships have a more difficult time taking schooling seriously. When I was growing up, my parents' struggles to regain the middle-class lifestyle they had enjoyed in Egypt were painfully obvious. Again, neither they nor their friends ever lamented their lot—they did what they had to do, and what generations of Jews before them had done, to give the next generation the best chance possible at a better life. It could not have been clearer to me or my brother that our chance lay in education. By the time I was in high school, all I could see ahead of me was years and years of education, and indeed that is what I and many of my friends with similar backgrounds experienced.

None of us were necessarily exemplars of humanity. We were driven by immigrant anxiety. I may very well have made a wonderful life for myself in what my mother refers to as the "heaven forbid" professions, such as art history or English literature, but I was too scared to take the chance. Some may think that I was too afraid of my parents to move in a direction unacceptable to them, but the reality is that I had internalized their experiences and anxieties, as well as their beliefs about what would serve me best in the long run. The trauma of immigration, acculturation, and anti-Semitism indelibly marked my parents' adult lives. Their experiences contributed to conversations, discussions, and arguments that inevitably focused us on our futures—our future educations and our future careers. We knew, for example, that a strong education would provide us with financial security and protect us from discrimination. "You can put a profession in your back pocket and go wherever you want to." "No one can take your degree away from you." These were the kinds of things my parents said to us and the kinds of things that high-achieving poor and minority children hear from their parents.

As I write these words, I can hear my students yelling at me: "Let children enjoy their childhoods!" "There will be plenty of time to learn life's harsh realities." "Why would you want to make kids grow up before they need to?" Believe me, there is nothing I want more for my own children, as well as everyone else's, than that they enjoy their childhoods. Yet having a happy childhood and being made aware of what adult life is like are not incompatible. Again, you need not make your children privy to your yearly income and monthly bank statements to get them to see that whatever you have as a family comes from hard work and sacrifice—hard work that you invested when you were a student and the hard work you put in now as a working adult.

> *Tess:* I was out all afternoon with Kate. She needed new running shoes and jeans. When we got what she needed, she asked if we could go to the crafts store to get a paint-by-numbers set. Well, I had spent a lot of money already, so I took out my wallet and asked her to count what was left. She counted $70.00. I told her that it needed to last me until Saturday, when I go to the bank to make my weekly withdrawal, so if we could find something for under $5.00, that would be OK.
>
> *Sandy:* You're kidding! You actually said that? My mother never would have done that. She would have thought that I would think she couldn't provide for us.

Giving children whatever they want, pretty much whenever they want it, is the equivalent of allowing them to experience only success in the classroom. A childhood of easily attained material benefits, like easily attained success, does not provide children with the experiences everyone needs to get through difficult situations. Tess saw a "teachable moment" in her seven-year-old's request for a trip to the crafts store. Moments like this, accumulated over a child's life, serve to reinforce the message that getting through life, like getting through school, takes patience, concerted effort, and the ability to delay gratification.

- Show your children, in word and in deed, that the material things they desire are not always easily attainable.

- Let your children experience the disappointment that comes with having to wait for, or never getting, the one special item they have wanted "their whole lives."

🌀 Know that it is OK for your children to be unhappy with you some of the time.

## Know the Difference: "Developmentally Appropriate" Versus Irresponsible Behavior

Look, I'm not making excuses for Cal. But the reality is that he's sixteen years old now, and his hormones are raging. Am I happy that he's gotten caught a few times leaving school in the middle of the day? Of course not. But he just can't seem to resist the temptation to test authority, mine and the school's. I can't pick his friends for him, and they're the ones who egg him on, especially Richie—it all comes from him, and I know it. I'm not gonna go nuts over this. It's developmentally appropriate. In fact, if he weren't doing stuff like this, I'd worry.

—*Rachel, Cal's mother*

There is no way I'm making any excuses for Richie's behavior. I don't care what his friends are thinking or doing, but they are not going to drag him down the path of skipping school and smoking in the bathroom. We probably should have seen this coming. He's been more defiant this year than ever before. Some of it is natural, I guess. He's sixteen, after all. But still, all it took was that one call from the principal, and it's a whole new ball game at home.

—*Sharon, Richie's mother*

Along with self-esteem, one of the more infamous myths recently perpetrated on parents is that acting out, misbehavior, disobedience, or whatever you wish to call it is both healthy and "developmentally appropriate." In other words, the kinds of behaviors that would have landed us in serious trouble as teenagers, such as refusing to do homework, cutting school, and experimenting with drugs have now been elevated to the status of a "normal" innate need, over which parents can exert little or no control. The underlying message is offensive to those students who go about their business with sincerity. As if it were not bad enough that we look down on students who excel in school, apparently we can now look down on students who don't get into trouble. For parents who are struggling with rebellious teenagers, this news comes as a great relief to some and a curse to others. I fear that those like Rachel, who feel relief, are deluding themselves.

All of us understand that adolescence is a time to test the limits, push the envelope, and otherwise spread wings more widely than is advisable. This makes for very stressful periods in the lives of many families. The most difficult—and most important—thing to do is to continue to be a *parent* and not try to be your teenager's *friend*. A certain degree of understanding is of course warranted, but, as I have said earlier, you need to make and adhere to crystal-clear rules about school. Unfortunately, the pathway to risk taking, including drugs, alcohol, and sexually transmitted diseases, often begins with what many parents consider relatively harmless acts of defiance, such as erratic grades and "forgetting" homework at school. Society's willingness to accept these kinds of irresponsible behaviors as developmentally appropriate indicators of healthy psychosocial growth gives some parents license to let go too early and too easily. Peer pressure, such as it is, then becomes much more enticing.

Getting their parents "off their backs" may be what many teenagers wish for in their angriest moments, but it is not what they truly want, as these teenagers point out:

> Don't give in to us all the time so you can be our
> friend. We have friends. What we need are parents

who set boundaries and keep them. We need
teachers and administrators to stop being our
classmates. We want them to be our teachers and
to teach. We want them to lead us, but don't
underestimate us; set the rules and carry them out.
No more threats as to what will happen if and when.

—*Jill, sixteen*

It is not good for parents to give us everything we
want. Say "no" to us. Don't bail us out of the trouble
we get ourselves into. When you do, that teaches us
that we don't have to be accountable for our bad
choices.

—*Tabitha, fifteen*

## Learn from Other Cultures

I explained to the Japanese teachers that some of my
very bright students are reluctant for other students
to know they are bright. Instead of aiming for their
best, they often go for the mediocre so they will be
accepted by their peers. American students respect
those who are good athletes while labeling the
scholastically able as "nerds." Often the good
students lives are made miserable. When I asked
the Japanese if they see this attitude in their classes,
they didn't understand. Their students respect those
who do well on the high school entrance exam.

—*Visiting high school teacher*
*and Fulbright scholar*

The cultural beliefs that help shape the higher achievement of
Asian and European students, as well as of American students of

differing cultural and ethnic descents, hold critical messages about respect, responsibility, and the obligations of children toward their parents, teachers, and one another. We need to take a step back to learn from others how we can prevail on peers to encourage each other's achievement rather than disparage one another about excelling in school.

Let me be clear: I am not joining the ranks of those who have argued that we need to become "more Japanese" or "more German" if we want our students to be better prepared for the technological challenges that lie ahead. Nor am I holding up any particular ethnic group in this country as a model for how all our students should think and behave. We are a unique society, shaped by a common culture that evolves with every successive wave of immigration. Yet the truth is that the educational scene abroad as well as in many ethnic and cultural groups in this country holds important lessons that we would be foolish to ignore:

- Education is a privilege, not a gratuity.
- Education is a responsibility, both personal and collective.
- Education is an obligation, not a casual agreement between children and parents.

I fear that these points may sound terribly Pollyannaish to many readers, but this broad outlook on schooling leads to classroom practices and learning strategies that foster mutual encouragement among students. For example, Japanese children take turns serving lunch out of platters and stockpots. All children work to keep their classrooms tidy and clean. This collective sense of obligation is evident in daily learning. When students work in groups, they are clear about their responsibilities and help one another achieve the group's goal, whether it is to find multiple ways to determine the area of an odd shape or to set personal goals for themselves and their classmates. Put another way, students have each other's support as they try to be the best students they can be.

You can find and replicate this kind of mutual support using a simple strategy that has been a part of higher education for a long time: the study group. Many educators have taken a keen interest in the fact that many students of Asian descent work in groups during and after school. They share notes, explain problems and their solutions to one another, and quiz one another in preparation for tests and exams. The overall higher achievement of these students has not gone unnoticed and has led some schools to create study groups for all students. Working in a study group is not cheating; it is cooperative learning in the best sense of the term. And it has the added benefit of easing the homework hassles of which I spoke in Chapter Four:

> I have this thing—call me crazy—but I need to have Amanda [eight] do her homework as soon as she gets home from school. I know she could do it later, but I'm neurotic. I can't enjoy my dinner and evening with my family if there is still homework to do. Well, you can imagine the endless arguments.
>
> The problem isn't Amanda; it's this culture of play dates. Everybody has play dates except Amanda, something I can certainly live with, but she's another story. She is so angry and sees us as being so incredibly unfair. So you know what I did? I told her that she could bring a friend home every day if she wanted, as long as they did their homework first thing.
>
> Of course, her friends' parents are thrilled to find homework done and checked when they pick their children up. Now I have three kids coming home every day. I sit the four of them down with a snack and their homework, and they've got a study group going.
>
> —*Grace, Amanda's mother*

I asked Grace if she felt put upon or taken advantage of. I wanted to know if she felt as though she were fulfilling other parents' responsibilities. After all, Grace is the one holding the homework bag while the parents in question get to go home to a relatively calm evening, freed from whatever homework "battles" they used to have. She understood my question but said that, selfishly, she prefers it this way because Amanda and the others learn more from one another than they do from working alone. And, in her own way, she has put an end to her own homework hassles.

# CHAPTER 8

# What You Say and Do Really Matters

We would like to get off this crazy treadmill, really we would. We both work, and we have a lot of stress in that part of our lives. We have three children, in the fourth, seventh, and ninth grades. Each brings us so much joy, and so much work, emotional and physical. Sometimes the sheer amount of homework is dizzying. I'll be honest with you, it's tough after a long day at work. But, for now at least, we've worked out a homework system that works. It's the other stuff that's killing us. The sports—games, practices— music lessons, ceramics, gymnastics . . . It just goes on and on. How did we get to this place? This is not what we imagined when we started our family.

*—Joshua, father of three*

As parents, we all share the same worries about our children's education: How can we best prepare them to face the rapidly changing world in which we live? The society in which they will come of age will be much more fast paced, competitive, and demanding than the one we came to inherit as children of the baby boom. We want to provide our children with the best possible education, but at the same time we recognize that education is not and cannot be the only focus in their lives. Children, like adults, need a balance in their daily activities. In some ways, children need this sense of balance more than we do, because this is their time to explore the different interests they have. All of us who are raising or teaching youngsters are mindful of how difficult and complex it can be to balance the competing desires we harbor for our children.

Joshua, the father whose remarks open this chapter, is expressing frustrations that are common to many of us, yet the tone of his comments seems to indicate that he feels at a loss, that somehow he and his wife woke up one morning to find that, overnight, their lives as a family of five had become incredibly complicated and stressful. He is speaking as though his family life is beyond his control, but this is far from being the case. He and his wife can indeed find the balance they and their children need. The treadmill can indeed be stopped long enough for his family to get off and reassess its lifestyle. Those of you who are feeling similarly pressured to be all, do all, and give all to your children need to know that you have the capacity to give your children profound gifts that will last them a lifetime. I am not speaking of team memberships or music lessons or excursions to museums or trips away from home. The gifts of which I speak are not material in nature—they are the building blocks of motivation and academic achievement, and they are each related to the other. They are not easy to give; each involves a great deal of *sustained* time, energy, effort, and patience on our parts.

## The Gift of Your Example

The things you say and do about schooling and learning really do matter. Over time, all your comments become interpreted by your children as general beliefs or attitudes toward education. You cannot mock high-achieving students, even in jest, and expect your children to value academic excellence, whether it be theirs or that of their peers. You cannot deride your children's teachers, even in what you might consider the slightest way, and expect your children to hold them in high regard. You cannot be complacent in the face of poor grades and expect your children to take their education seriously.

Expressing admiration for students who do well in school, showing respect for teachers, and being concerned about poor grades do not guarantee that your children will make your orientation toward learning their own, but they do set a general tone of esteem for intellectual pursuits. Set this tone early by preparing your children to be students. Share your love of books and reading with your children. Read to them and have them see you reading, whether it be for work or for enjoyment. Take them to your library, borrow books, read them, and teach your children to care for them. Gradually build for each of your children their own collection of books—their own personal library. Set aside an area in your home that you call their "study." Keep books, paper, crayons, pencils, children's scissors, and such in their study. All these things may seem very small, but they are profound in their influence. It is in these small and subtle ways, accumulated over the years, that your children will come to realize that scholarship is important in your family.

## The Gift of Your Involvement

You need to know what is going on in your children's daily lives at school. A passing familiarity with homework is not enough to provide you with information that can be truly useful to you when your children begin to encounter problems, whether academic or social. You do not need to know *so* much about your children's classrooms that you become an expert in elementary and secondary curricula. Yet you *do* need to know enough of the content so that the teacher's expectations make sense to you, so that you can either provide help or find help when your children need it, and so that you can advocate for your children when things in the classroom do not seem to be going well.

Your children's social development is no less important than their academic development. Of course you will come to know your children's friends and their families. As much as your schedule allows, get to know the other children in the classroom. Doing so gives you a sense of the classroom dynamics—who likes whom, who dislikes whom, how the class members live and work together. This kind of information is invaluable as your children learn to negotiate the sometimes tricky world of peers. The more you know about your children's social scene, the more you can be of help when conflicts arise. When you let your children see that you are involved in their school lives, whatever form your involvement takes, you let them know that what is happening in school really matters to you, that you care about what and how they are learning and how they are getting along with the other adults and children in their lives.

## The Gift of High Expectations

Expect your children to do their very best in school. Barring serious learning difficulties or mental retardation, all children can reach their potential. They are unlikely to do so, however, if we limit our encouragement to such platitudes as, "We expect much more from you." It is so much more encouraging for your children to hear *how* you believe they can meet your expectations. Give them several concrete examples of the steps they can take to improve their performance, and let them know that you are there to guide them if they want your help. For example, if the quality of your children's writing is an issue, go over the basics of story composition; teach them how to break an assignment down into manageable pieces, and how to put the pieces together into their story; reinforce the importance of first and final drafts; and the like.

It is often said that children will rise to the standards to which we hold them. This is true but does not happen magically. Those children who have our academic support, emotional encouragement, and the benefit of our patience will most certainly become academically proficient.

Clearly, some children have a heavier load to bear than others.

In general, children's home lives are bound to be more stressful if they lose a parent through divorce or death, if they experience a parent's remarriage and perhaps become stepsiblings, if there is illness or addiction in the family, or if their families suffer an economic downturn. These are (sadly) only some of the trying experiences children can live through, experiences that make many parents and teachers want to lighten their academic load. As well-intentioned as these sentiments may be, children do not need our pity—they need our continued commitment to support and teach them. It is precisely during such periods in children's lives that we should be the most vigilant about maintaining high standards for their school achievement.

By all means, allow children to express their emotions. The knowledge that they can confide in a caring adult is a great comfort to many children. Of course, be understanding of their troubles and worries. We do no children any favors, least of all those who are at a disadvantage, when we lower expectations for their school performance. When we lower our expectations, we are depriving our children of opportunities to learn. As I have said in earlier chapters, children are very savvy and know when they are being assigned easier work relative to their peers. The knowledge that they are being treated differently than others can make any student doubt his or her abilities, a state of affairs that virtually guarantees motivational problems, including the tendency to fall apart at the first sign of difficulty.

After many years of arguing with my students, as well as with parents and teachers, I concede that some children are "smarter" than others in some areas, but this neither bothers nor discourages me. High intelligence, in and of itself, is not the be-all and end-all. In fact, knowing that they have high intelligence can be a curse for many students, who come to believe that they should *never* have to struggle or be confused and thus are at a loss when they experience difficulty. From where I sit in the debate over intelligence, it is more of a punishment than a relief to know that one has a high IQ. I would much rather have my own children be persistent and diligent than have high IQs.

## The Gift of Seeing Effort as a Virtue

I have talked earlier in this book about the powerful influence you have on your children's developing beliefs about effort and ability. Above all else, be mindful of how you speak about what it takes to do well in school. Let your children know that you believe not in their ability per se, but rather in their ability to master even the most difficult work. Students do not need to believe that they are the smartest in their school or in their grade or even in their classroom. They need to think that they have the ability to learn and that disciplined effort can compensate for whatever lack of natural ability they may think they have. You can encourage this belief with each piece of advice, each pointer, each strategy that you provide for dealing with difficulty. This consistent message, delivered throughout childhood and adolescence, will lead to a clearer understanding that trying hard does not imply a lack of ability but rather can open new ways of learning and understanding. The knowledge that they may very well *not* understand a concept the first time they encounter it comes as a great relief to many children. You convey this important lesson every time you go over your children's homework with them, teach them a new skill, or help them study for a test. Of course, neither you nor they will be impervious to comparisons with other students. Nonetheless, stress the *processes* involved in learning rather than the end product alone. In other words, speak to your children about the steps they need to take in order to do well in school.

## The Gift of "Learned" Challenge

Some children are naturally drawn to challenge. Others need a little nudge to try something a little different, something that might be a little hard. Still others are terrified at the thought of attempting the kind of problem they cannot in advance know they will be able to solve. The expression *Nothing ventured, nothing gained* says it all. Take every opportunity that comes your way to show your children how much you learn from your own mistakes. I am not suggesting you dance for joy when you discover that you have made a monumental error in balancing your checkbook. By all means, express your anger and disappointment with yourself, for these are natural reactions. What you choose to do next will demonstrate to your children how well you capitalize on your mistakes. Strategize aloud about how you can avoid making such an error ever again, and follow through on your own ideas. For example, make separate files for your different credit card invoices, your bank statements, and rent or mortgage payments.

This kind of approach to your own foibles makes it easier for you to show your children that taking a chance on something new can be exciting, even if mistakes are in the offing. Children who live in fear of mistakes need to see that others survive and even learn something as a result of blunders. You need to help them learn, to experience their own survival in the wake of mistakes and mishaps. It is in these ways that children can learn to cope with, if not embrace, academic challenge. And as I have mentioned elsewhere, do not be lulled into thinking that "smart" children are immune to these kinds of debilitating concerns. In many cases, it is *because* they are smart and have had little experience with mistakes that they shy away from opportunities to learn something new.

## The Gift of Academic Struggle

Most children and adults will tell you that the success they most value is the one that was the hardest to earn. In my high school, virtually every student who passed through Mr. Ogobwe's chemistry lab will tell you that they hated him and everything about his class. In the next breath, though, they will tell you that they learned the most from him, the school's most demanding teacher, and that if they had to do it again they would not think of studying chemistry with any other teacher.

And so, as painful as it is, you must let your children struggle through confusion and difficulty. Learning to manage a difficult subject area is like learning to put the groceries away, an "informal" task I described in Chapter Three. At first, it is a daunting and confusing job. If you allow them to, your children will make many mistakes as they learn to classify and categorize household items. Over time and with repeated experiences, they will work out a system that makes sense to you and them. But every directive on your part robs them of chances to work out the kinks for themselves.

The same principle applies to "formal" learning, the kind of learning children do in school. Struggling through a difficult problem is the single most important way in which children learn to strategize in the face of obstacles. Every problem that you solve for your children, every answer you dole out, represents a missed opportunity for them to deepen their understanding of whatever it is that is giving them trouble. By all means, be their scaffold as they construct meaning out of unfamiliar assignments, but leave it at that. Have faith that over time and with your guidance, your children will become more and more skilled at climbing over academic obstacles.

## The Gift of Sharing Your Struggles

Many parents feel it is natural to protect their children from knowing about the kinds of difficulties and struggles they themselves had to endure while they were growing up. After all, childhood is supposed to be a happy time, and some parents believe that openness about past hardships would be too painful for children to bear. There is an important benefit, though, that comes from sharing with your children stories about the obstacles you and your partner have had to overcome. It is a profound lesson for your children to learn that you had unpleasant and even agonizing experiences while you were growing up. The value in such family stories is that, accumulated over time, they demonstrate to your children that material and psychological advantages cannot be taken for granted. This knowledge can make them more appreciative of what they have and more positive about the educational road that lies ahead.

In this context, it is interesting that more-affluent teenagers believe that their lives are harder and more stressful than were their parents' lives when *they* were teenagers. In contrast, lower-income teenagers perceive their lives as being much easier than their parents' lives were. These excerpts from a recent survey are very revealing:

> "I think everything's gotten harder since my parents were growing up," said Molly Wilhelm, 15, of Lakeville, Minn. "Back then, I think everyone was more equal, but now, because there's so much more offered in styles of clothes and stuff, we all want to fit in. I think my parents had more free time, and the world isn't as safe as it was in their day. It's more common for kids to do drugs and all that stuff. Education gets progressively harder as people learn more, and there's more to cover. And now that there's more technology, they expect more out of us.

> "I think it's easier now because of technology," said Ariel Garcia of Opa-Locka, Fla. "When you want to do a report, you just look at the Internet, you don't have to go to the library. Cars have air conditioning now, so you're comfortable. There's microwaves, so it's easy to cook. My dad had it much harder. He's Dominican, and he was in the Navy. That's tough. I would never go into the Navy. Those rich kids, they don't appreciate what their parents do for them. The money just goes right through their hands."

Affluent teenagers appear to see the benefits in their lives as curses; lower-income students see them as blessings. Of course, we cannot know the extent to which their different perceptions are a direct result of knowing (or not knowing) about their parents' past struggles. Nonetheless, there is something to be said for doling out appropriate doses of reality at appropriate times in your children's lives.

## The Gift of Prioritization

By definition, there can be only one top priority in a list of priorities. Where our children's development is concerned, education must be the one and only priority. This does not mean that we abandon all things extra-curricular, but it does imply that you have to be willing to make difficult choices when you are confronted with conflicts or dilemmas. I have a sense that too many parents have become afraid to be parents to their children. Instead, they want to be their children's friends. As we all know, the relationship between children and their parents is inherently unequal. We are in a position of authority relative to our children: we are older than our children, we see the world through a completely different lens than they do, and we are the ones in the position of acting on what we believe to be their best interests.

In this context, we must consider activities that fall outside the realm of schoolwork as *privileges*. Participation in outside activities is not an entitlement. Rather, it is something to which we give our *conditional* consent. We need to make it clear to our children that we are delighted to have them participate in sports or learn to play an instrument or take art classes, *provided their schoolwork does not suffer*. I have no problem whatsoever with our children getting angry at us for setting limits that we believe need to be set. That is our job, our obligation to them. As far as I am concerned, be as mean as you like. Your children are allowed to disagree with your priorities; by all means, acknowledge their anger. When you set clear priorities for yourself and your children, you model for them strategies for setting priorities for themselves as they get older.

The last thing you have to fear is that your children will not be well-rounded. This term has come to mean so many things to so many people that it has almost no meaning at all. Well-roundedness is not an either-or proposition. With the exception of extreme circumstances in which parents push their children to excel in one domain to the exclusion of others, all children are well-rounded in their own ways. Are students who are more thinly spread out *more* well-rounded? Some parents may think so, but a lot of anecdotal evidence suggests that many children suffer under the weight of overcommitment and overscheduling. Many are the newspaper articles or Sunday magazine essays that speak of children *begging* to be pulled out of planned activities. More is not better; it's just more, and potentially debilitating at that.

It is never too late to set boundaries for academic and social behavior, but the sooner you do so the better. Establishing clear-cut rules later in the game just makes it harder on everyone, children as well as parents. Be assured that no one can dictate how rigid you should be in adhering to your rules. The best bet is to be as consistent as possible, while recognizing *rare* times when it would be appropriate to bend your rules just a bit. You are the best judge of what will work for you and your children. In this context, understand that treating each of your children *fairly* does not necessarily imply treating them *exactly the same way.* Your children's differing temperaments present themselves from the day they are born, and what works for one will not necessarily work for another. A child who is inconsistent in completing her homework assignments needs more supervision than a child who does his work on time. The first may cry foul, but you need to let her know how and why it is that you are following her daily schooling a little more closely than you are her brother's.

## The Gift of Obligation

Most people think of obligation as a burden or constraint, not as a gift. Yet, in my mind, your children are better off in the long run for understanding and accepting that they have daily obligations, the most important of which is to do well in school. They need to know that you work very hard to fulfill your responsibilities to those with whom you live and work. In the same way, they should see that they have an obligation to you, your family, and their teachers to do what is expected of them in the best way they know how, to ask for help when they need it, and to be responsible for their work. Talk about school being your children's job, inasmuch as your work, be it in or out of the home, is *your* job. When appropriate opportunities present themselves, let your children know what your work involves, how hard you work, and the people with whom you collaborate to get your job done. Liken your work to their own work as students. In no way do I feel it is appropriate to unload all your problems on your children. Yet I do believe that at a certain point around mid-childhood, they need to have a sense of the sacrifices you make in the service of your family. A little bit of guilt can go a long way in helping keep children on track.

## The Gift of Resiliency

When you consistently provide a supportive and disciplined environment for learning, you give your children the gift of resiliency against setbacks and failures. To be sure, this resiliency does not come into being overnight; it develops over years: years of patient and guided teaching, years filled with a multitude of encounters—big and small—with success and failure, setbacks and breakthroughs, disappointment and mastery. It is neither easy nor straightforward to encourage strengths of character that will help your children see their way through difficult experiences—in this regard, we all are on uncharted water. That some children turn out more resilient than others may be due as much, if not more, to their personalities as to their parents' efforts. Yet for every child whose temperament is such that she rebounds quickly after failure, there is a child who needs to be carefully guided toward beliefs and behaviors that will make her more resilient and less prone to fall apart when things do not go her way.

## The Gift of Competence

Competence cannot be orchestrated; it must be earned. Parents who protect their children from mistakes and failure do them a profound disservice, for children must experience failure in order to learn how to cope with it. Children do not soak up strategies for dealing with difficulty and challenge by osmosis. They must experience stressful assignments, projects, and the like in order for them to develop a deeper understanding of what it takes to get out of an academic jam. There can be no such thing as homework that is not stressful. On the contrary, learning that comes easily is not learning at all—it is simply doing.

Be assured that academic challenges enhance rather than diminish self-esteem. Students feel incredibly good about themselves when they finally understand something that has been a tremendous source of confusion and frustration for them. I have no doubt that proponents of self-esteem have got it all wrong. Children do not need to feel good about themselves in order to learn. They need to *learn* in order to feel good about themselves.

## Getting Back on Track

Our children are seriously deficient in the skills they will need to survive in this new century, and we are incredibly complacent about the educational crisis that is before us. We have a lot of hard work ahead of us, and we need to acknowledge that the responsibility for getting our children back on track is as much ours as it is our children's teachers. They cannot do their jobs well without our consistent involvement in our children's schooling. With this in mind, we need to stop thinking about our children's lives as if they were divided into a life *in* school and a life *outside* school. Children have *one* life, an *integrated* life that can be as rich as you like with scholarship, religion, athleticism, the arts, and community activism. However, the responsibility for setting priorities in your children's lives rests squarely with you. You are the best judge of how many weekly obligations your children can tolerate. More important, you are the final arbiter of how many obligations you feel are *appropriate*. Your children may very well be able to participate in far more activities than you feel are warranted. Remember that you are *parents*, not friends, to your children. Do not worry about whether or not your children are well-rounded enough. They will always find non-academic interests that will fill them with joy and passion. Do not worry about whether or not they feel good enough about themselves. They, like us, will always feel good about themselves in some areas but not in others, and these areas will change as your children change and develop. Place your faith in their education—make it your top priority—for this is where the promise of knowledge and prosperity lies.

# Appendix: Helpful Questions to Ask Yourself and Your Children's Teachers

There are many ways to promote positive beliefs about learning and support our children's education at home. As we all know, it can be difficult at times to determine whether our efforts are having the impact we intend. We offer these questions as a way for you to think about your own perspective on your children's schooling. In addition, we provide suggestions for asking your children's teachers about their own perspectives on how your children are approaching learning in their classrooms. These questions may be particularly useful when you prepare for parent-teacher conferences.

## Chapter 1: Challenging Our Assumptions

Ask yourself:

1. How much importance am I placing on my children's education relative to other activities in their lives?

2. Are my children clear about our family's priorities?

3. Do I feel comfortable letting my children struggle with appropriately challenging work, possibly at the expense of their immediate happiness?

This appendix was authored by Beth A. Delamater. The helpful feedback of Anne Marie Osiecki is gratefully acknowledged.

Ask the teacher:

1. Do my children show respect for you in the things they say and do in the classroom?

2. Do you think my children are putting an appropriate amount of effort into their schoolwork? Is their level of effort consistent?

3. Do you think my children are being challenged by the class work? Is there an area where you think I should supplement some of the work that you assign?

## Chapter 2: Talking to Your Children About School

Ask yourself:

1. What do I really think about my children's mistakes: Do I see them as opportunities to learn new things, or as evidence that they might not be smart enough?

2. Do I talk to my children about how trying hard can maximize their abilities, and actually make them smarter?

3. Do I offer my children specific strategies that they can use to work their way out of confusion or difficulty?

Ask the teacher:

1. Do the assignments provide room for my children to make mistakes and learn how to improve their work?

2. How do my children react when they make mistakes? Do you think they feel embarrassed or ashamed? Or do you think they take it in stride and focus on figuring out the right answer? What do you say and do when you make a mistake in the classroom?

3. Do you think my children are diligent enough in their efforts to get their work done correctly, or do you find that they are careless? What do you think I can do at home to help them be more organized?

## Chapter 3: Supporting Achievement at Home

Ask yourself:

1. How important do I think it is to involve my children in daily activities at home, such as tidying up, sorting the laundry, or putting away the groceries?
2. When I help my children do their homework, to what extent am I providing hints and ideas, as opposed to providing the answers?
3. Do I ask my children to imagine their futures? Do I talk about what steps are involved in getting them to reach their goals?

Ask the teacher:

1. How much active involvement do my children have in their learning? Do they ask questions? Do they seem excited about coming up with creative solutions to problems?
2. Do you think my children have good study habits, or should I keep a closer eye on them to make sure they complete their assignments?
3. Do you think my children have high enough expectations for their schoolwork? Do you think they are too hard on themselves, or do you think they need to push themselves a little more?

## Chapter 4: Dealing with Homework

Ask yourself:

1. Do I view homework as something that can help my children develop good study habits, or do I tend to see homework as more of an intrusion on my family's life?

2. Do I make it clear to my children that they have to complete their homework on time, even if it might be unpleasant or time consuming?

3. Do my children know that I expect them to do their homework before they do other activities? Have I clearly communicated the consequences should they not complete their work before doing other things?

Ask the teacher:

1. Are my children completing their homework consistently, and on time?

2. Can you give me a sense of how long it should take my children to complete particular assignments? This will help me know whether they are spending too much or too little time on their projects.

3. What can we do at home to make sure my children are doing their work? Can you suggest some strategies we can use to monitor their schoolwork and to hold them accountable for work they do not finish? What are the consequences in your classroom if children do not complete their work on time?

## Chapter 5: Working with the Teacher's Values

Ask yourself:

1. Do I sometimes question the teacher's authority in front of my children?

2. Do I try to help my children see the teacher's perspective when they complain, or do I join them in their outrage?

3. Have I thought through what I really value in my children's education, and whether or not their current teachers seem to hold similar values?

Ask the teacher:

1. What is your philosophy about grading and evaluation? How can I know if my children are living up to your expectations?

2. Do you group the children by ability in some subjects, such as reading? Do you think my children are in the right ability group? How can I help them prepare so they'll be ready for more challenging work—perhaps in a higher track? Or how can I help them see that being in the top group isn't the be-all and end-all—that it is more important to be in the group that is best for their learning?

3. Do my children have difficulty following the day's routines? If so, what do you think is going on? What do you think I can do at home to get them back on track?

### Chapter 6: Balancing Extra-Curricular Interests with Academic Obligations

Ask yourself:

1. Have I managed to keep school the top priority in our household, even as I've allowed my children's interests in outside activities to flourish?

2. Have I clearly communicated the consequences for my children if their schoolwork suffers? Am I really willing to follow through with these consequences (for example, taking away activities)?

3. Do I show as much pride and excitement over my children's academic accomplishments as I do over their athletic or artistic progress?

Ask the teacher:

1. Do you think that my children have a reasonable balance between their schoolwork and extra-curricular activities?

2. Would you let me know when my children are doing particularly well in their schoolwork? I want to be sure to praise them and show how important their doing well in school is to me.

3. What do you think are my children's strengths, and how do you think I can encourage their development in those areas?

## Chapter 7: Confronting Negative Peer Pressure

Ask yourself:

1. Do I tell my children stories about my own schooling? Do my stories relay how much of an impact education has on everyone's life?

2. Do I talk to my children about their future goals, and help them develop a vision of what their future lives might look like?

3. Do I give my children enough structure to withstand the influence of friends who may not care as much about school as I do?

Ask the teacher:

1. How do you respond when students get into the "anti-achievement" stance? What can I do and say at home to counter the notion that it's cool to goof off?

2. Do you think my children are proud of themselves when they do well in school? Do you get the sense that they might be embarrassed when they do well? Do they downplay their academic accomplishments?

3. Can you suggest other students my child might form a support or study group with? Are there particular students they like to work with in the classroom?

## Chapter 8: What You Say and Do Really Matters

Ask yourself:

1. Are my children doing too much outside of school? Is the pace of our family life faster than I would like it to be?

2. Am I setting a positive example for how to think about learning specifically, and education generally?

3. Have I taken enough time to get to know my children's school and their teachers? Would I know who to go to if a problem arose, or would I feel out of the loop?

Ask the teacher:

1. Given my own constraints and obligations, how can I become more involved with your classroom and my children's learning? What can I do to help you?

2. My children's education is truly at the top of my priority list. Can you let me know if you feel that other activities or obligations are interfering with their schoolwork?

3. I want my children to be willing to struggle with material that is appropriately challenging or difficult. Would you let me know if you think they are avoiding difficult work or not speaking out because they are afraid to make mistakes?

# Notes

## Chapter 1

p. 1

". . . competence . . . increasingly at risk": Beaton, A., and others. *Mathematics Achievement in the Middle School Years: IEA's Third International Mathematics and Science Study.* Boston College: Center for the Study of Testing, Evaluation, and Educational Policy, 1996; Stevenson, H., and Lee, S. "Contexts of Achievement: A Study of American, Chinese, and Japanese Children." *Monographs for the Society for Research in Child Development,* 1990, 55(1–2, ser. no. 221).

p. 3

"Poverty, single parenthood . . .": Pallas, A., Natriello, G., and McDill, E. "The Changing Nature of the Disadvantaged Population: Current Dimensions and Future Trends." *Educational Researcher,* 1989, 18, 16–22.

p. 3

"Increasing self-esteem . . .": Neuman, S. "The Negative Consequences of the Self-Esteem Movement." *Alberta Journal of Educational Research,* 1992, 38, 251–253.

p. 6

". . . reason, analyze, and synthesize . . .": Vygotsky, L. *Thought and Language.* (E. Hanfman and G. Bakar, eds. and trans.). Cambridge, Mass.: MIT Press, 1962.

p. 7
". . . double-edged sword": Covington, M. V., and Omelich, C. L. "Effort: The Double-Edged Sword in School Achievement." *Journal of Educational Psychology*, 1979, *71*, 169–182.
p. 7
"Children's beliefs . . .": Bempechat, J., London, P., and Dweck, C. "Children's Conceptions of Ability in Major Domains: An Interview and Experimental Study." *Child Study Journal*, 1991, *21*, 11–36.
p. 9
"increase in scheduled activities . . .": Ferguson, A. "Inside the Crazy Culture of Kids Sports." *Newsweek*, July 12, 1999, vol. 154, no. 2, pp. 52–60.
p. 9
". . . my colleague Nancy . . .": Bempechat, J. *Against the Odds: How "At Risk" Students Exceed Expectations.* San Francisco: Jossey-Bass, 1998. All names in this vignette are disguised to ensure confidentiality.

## Chapter 2

p. 14
"The things we say . . .": Bempechat, London, and Dweck (1991).
p. 19
"Most of us believe . . .": Dweck, C., and Bempechat, J. "Children's Theories of Intelligence: Consequences for Learning." In S. G. Paris, G. M. Olson, and H. W. Stevenson (eds.), *Learning and Motivation in the Classroom.* Hillsdale, N.J.: Erlbaum, 1983.
p. 19
". . . intelligence as *limited* and *limiting* . . .": Dweck and Bempechat (1983).
p. 24
". . . the harder they *have* to try . . .": Nicholls, J. "Conceptions of Ability and Achievement Motivation: A Theory and Its Implications for Education." In S. Paris, G. Olson, and H. Stevenson (eds.),

*Learning and Motivation in the Classroom*. Hillsdale, N.J.: Erlbaum, 1983.

p. 24

"By the fourth or fifth grades . . .": Bempechat, London, and Dweck (1991).

p. 25

"In this kind of atmosphere . . .": Nicholls, J. *The Competitive Ethos and Democratic Education*. Cambridge, Mass.: Harvard University Press, 1989.

p. 26

"Students who see luck . . .": Weiner, B. "Integrating Social and Personal Theories of Achievement Strivings." *Review of Educational Research*, 1994, *64*, 557–573.

p. 27

"Much of the educational research . . .": Stevenson, H., Chen, C., and Lee, S. "Mathematics Achievement of Chinese, Japanese, and American Children: Ten Years Later." *Science*, 1993, *259*, 53–58.

p. 32

". . . Sophie would be modeling . . .": Rogoff, B. *Apprenticeship in Thinking: Cognitive Development in a Social Context*. New York: Oxford University Press, 1990.

p. 33

"Girls do much better . . .": Wolleat, P., Pedro, J., Becker, A., and Fennema, E. "Sex Differences in High School Students' Causal Attributions of Performance in Mathematics." *Journal for Research in Mathematics*, 1980, *11*, 356–366; Stipek, D. J., and Gralinski, J. H. "Gender Differences in Children's Achievement-Related Beliefs and Emotional Responses to Success and Failure in Mathematics." *Journal of Educational Psychology*, 1991, *83*, 361–371; Eccles (Parsons), J., Adler, T., and Meece, J. "Sex Differences in Achievement: A Test of Alternative Theories." *Journal of Personality and Social Psychology*, 1984, *46*, 26–43.

p. 33

". . . young women are very much absent . . .": Hilton, T., Hsia, J., Solorzano, D., and Benton, N. *Persistence in Science of High Ability Minority Students*. Princeton, N.J.: Educational Testing Service,

1989; Reyes, L., and Stanic, G. "Race, Sex, and Socioeconomic Status and Mathematics." *Journal for Research in Mathematics Education*, 1984, *15*, 154–164.

p. 34

". . . poor or failing grades from their boys . . .": Holloway, S. "The Relationship of Mothers' Beliefs to Children's Mathematics Achievement: Some Effects of Sex Differences." *Merrill-Palmer Quarterly*, 1986, *32*, 231–250.

## Chapter 3

p. 41

". . . earlier is better . . .": Elkind, D. *Ties That Stress: The New Family Imbalance*. Cambridge, Mass.: Harvard University Press, 1994.

p. 44

"Exactly how we go about. . .": Hess, R., and Shipman, V. "Early Experience and the Socialization of Cognitive Modes in Children." *Child Development*, 1965, *36*, 869–886.

p. 45

"The overall goal . . .": Rogoff (1990).

p. 48

". . . we act much like a *scaffold* . . .": Rogoff (1990); Rogoff, B., and Gardner, W. "Adult Guidance of Everyday Cognition." In B. Rogoff and J. Lave (eds.), *Everyday Cognition: Its Development in Social Context*. Cambridge, Mass.: Harvard University Press, 1984.

p. 52

"One thing is clear . . .": Garmezy, N. "Stress-Resistant Children: A Search for Positive Factors." In J. Stevenson (ed.), *Recent Research in Developmental Psychopathology*. New York: Pergamon Press, 1985.

p. 55

"Many studies of high-achieving . . .": Kao, G., and Tienda, M. "Optimism and Achievement: The Educational Performance of Immigrant Youth." *Social Science Quarterly*, 1995, *76*, 1–19.

p. 55

"Many children are surprised . . .": Graham, S., and Barker, G. "Developmental Study of Praise and Blame as Attributional Cues." *Developmental Psychology*, 1987, 79, 62–66.

p. 56

"But what's a bad grade . . .": Woo, E. "California's Perilous Slide; Language, Culture: How Schools Cope. Home Life Plays a Crucial Role in Students' Success or Faiure." *Los Angeles Times*, May 18, 1998, p. R1.

p. 57

"Students who have a farther-reaching . . .": Nuttin, J. *Future Time Perspective and Motivation: Theory and Research Methods*. Hillsdale, N.J.: Erlbaum, 1985.

## Chapter 4

p. 60

". . . heated public debates . . .": Begley, S. "Homework Doesn't Help." *Newsweek*, Mar. 30, 1998, p. 50.

p. 60

". . . our children's academic achievement . . .": Beaton and others (1996).

p. 61

"There was blood . . .": "Homework Doesn't Help." *Newsweek*, Mar. 30, 1998, p. 50.

p. 61

". . . educators believed that homework . . .": Cooper, H. *Homework*. White Plains, N.Y.: Longman, 1989.

p. 62

" . . . data on the underachievement of American . . ." Stevenson, H. W., Lee, S., and Stigler, J. W. "Mathematics Achievement of Chinese, Japanese, and American Children." *Science*, 1986, 231, 693–699.

p. 64
"Observers of educational trends . . .": Elkind, D. *The Hurried Child: Growing up Too Fast Too Soon*. Reading, Mass.: Addison-Wesley, 1988.

p. 64
". . . given that urban children . . .": National Educational Goals Report. *The Core Report*. Washington, D.C.: National Educational Goals Panel, 1995.

p. 64
". . . supporting their children's education . . .": Reese, L., Balzano, S., Gallimore, R., and Goldenberg, C. *The Concept of "Educaciòn": Latino Family Values and American Schooling*. (Forthcoming.)

p. 65
"In one early study . . .": Stevenson, Lee, and Stigler (1986).

p. 65
"The Third International . . .": Beaton and others (1996).

p. 66
Bulleted notes on homework: Cooper (1989).

p. 68
". . . these demands become increasingly complex . . .": Eccles, J. "Expectancies, Values, and Academic Behaviors." In J. Spence (ed.), *Achievement and Achievement Motives: Psychological and Social Approaches*. New York: Freeman, 1983.

p. 69
". . . the ability to do well in school . . .": Dweck and Bempechat (1983).

p. 73
"'It interrupts family life'": Goodavage, M. "Homework Ban Up for Vote." *USA Today*, Oct. 26, 1994, p. A1.

p. 73
"'Otherwise, we'd have no family time . . .'": Gold, D. "Some Question Homework's Merits." *Boston Globe*, May 17, 1998, p. D5.

p. 75
"It recalls the attitude . . .": Hess and Shipman (1965).

p. 75
". . . poor and minority families have many strengths . . .": Clark,

R. *Family Life and School Achievement: Why Poor Black Children Succeed and Fail.* Chicago: University of Chicago Press, 1983.

p. 76

"'It's a major difference'": Hurley, M. "The Three R's and Then Some." *Boston Globe*, Dec. 6, 1998.

p. 76

"Some educators push . . .": "Homework Doesn't Help." *Newsweek*, Mar. 30, 1998, p. 50.

p. 78

"By providing too much help . . .": Graham and Barker (1987).

## Chapter 5

p. 90

". . . grade inflation . . .": Hardy, L. "Grade Inflation." *American School Board Journal*, 1997, *184*, 28–30.

p. 94

". . . older students are peers . . .": Weiner, B., Graham, S., Stern, P., and Lawson, E. "Using Affective Cues to Infer Causal Thoughts." *Developmental Psychology*, 1982, *18*, 278–286.

p. 94

". . . mixed-age classrooms . . .": Roopnarine, J. "Social-Cognitive Behaviors and Playmate Preferences in Same-Age and Mixed-Age Classrooms over a 6–Month Period." *American Educational Research Journal*, 1991, *29*, 757–776.

p. 95

". . . extrinsic learning . . .": Greene, M., and Lepper, M. "Effects of Extrinsic Rewards on Children's Subsequent Intrinsic Interest." *Child Development*, 1974, *45*, 1141–1145.

p. 99

". . . poor . . . children are vastly over-represented . . .": Bryk, A., Lee, V., and Holland, P. *Catholic Schools and the Common Good.* Cambridge, Mass.: Harvard University Press, 1993.

p. 100

". . . ability grouping or tracking . . .": Oakes, J. *Keeping Track.* Cambridge, Mass.: Harvard University Press, 1985.

p. 101

". . . the need to reach out to parents . . .": Epstein, J. "Toward a Theory of Family-School Connections: Teacher Practices and Parent Involvement." In K. Hurrelmann, F. Kaufmann, and F. Losel (eds.), *Social Intervention: Potential and Constraints*. Hawthorne, N.Y.: Walter de Gruyter, 1987.

p. 104

"The beliefs you share with your children . . .": Sigel, I., McGillicuddy-DeLisi, A., and Goodnow, J. "Introduction to the Second Edition." In I. Sigel, A. McGillicuddy-DeLisi, and J. Goodnow (eds.), *Parental Belief Systems: The Psychological Consequences for Children*. (2nd ed.) Hillsdale, N.J.: Erlbaum, 1992.

## Chapter 6

p. 109

". . . multiple stressors . . .": Furstenberg, F. "Coming of Age in a Changing Family System." In S. Feldman and G. Elliott (eds.), *At the Threshold: The Developing Adolescent*. Cambridge, Mass.: Harvard University Press, 1990.

p. 110

". . . a typical afternoon . . .": Carroll, M. "Soccer and Baseball Square Off: Coaches Compete for Fields; Parents Scramble." *Boston Globe*, May 19, 1996.

p. 111

"'. . . an injustice to your kid'": Ferguson, A. "Inside the Crazy Culture of Kids Sports." *Newsweek*, July 12, 1999, vol. 154, no. 2, pp. 52–60.

p. 112

"'Even in the most intense programs . . .'": *Time* (1999).

p. 112

"'We've led a lot of people astray . . .'": Johnson, K. "The Self-Esteem Theory Loses Respect." *Portland Oregonian*, May 27, 1998, p. E13.

p. 113
"The self-esteem 'movement' . . .": Neuman (1992).

p. 113
". . . self-esteem varies . . .": Marsh, H. "Relations Among Dimensions of Self-Attribution, Dimensions of Self-Concept, and Academic Achievement." *Journal of Educational Psychology*, 1984, 76, 1291–1308.

p. 114
". . . through social promotion . . .": Rothstein, R. "Where Is Lake Wobegon, Anyway? The Controversy Surrounding Social Promotion." *Phi Delta Kappan*, 1998, 80, 195–198.

p. 121
". . . overscheduled and over-programmed . . .": Leonard, M. "Where Are the Kids? As More Kids Get Overbooked, Play Gives Way to Achievement." *Boston Globe*, Apr. 19, 1998, p. G1.

p. 121
". . . as these students attest": Powers, J. "Crash Course: As the Scramble to get into a Selective College Grows Tougher, Is It Any Wonder That High School Seniors Are Feeling More and More Overwhelmed?" *Boston Globe* (Sunday Magazine), Mar. 31, 1996.

p. 122
"'You can hire consultants . . .'": Powers, J. "Crash Course: As the Scramble to Get into a Selective College Grows Tougher, Is It Any Wonder That High School Seniors Are Feeling More and More Overwhelmed?" *Boston Globe* (Sunday Magazine), Mar. 31, 1996.

p. 123
"'What students bring to college . . .'": Samuelson, R. J. "The Worthless Ivy League?" *Newsweek*, Nov. 1, 1999.

p. 126
"'There is no correlation . . .'": Tye, L. and Romano, R. "Excellence Comes at a Price: Many Top Athletes and Their Parents Face Hard Choices." *Boston Globe*, Sept. 29, 1997, p. A1.

p. 127
". . . overuse injuries and reinjuries . . .": Jones, R. "Playing It Safe." *American School Board Journal*, 1997, 184, 22–24.

## Chapter 7

p. 129

Bumper stickers in opening epigraphs: cited in Schreiber, L. C. "Bumper Sticker Stings—and Reveals." *Boston Globe*, Oct. 26, 1997, p. N10.

p. 131

". . . intelligence has many components . . .": Gardner, H. *Frames of Mind*. New York: Basic Books, 1983.

p. 131

". . . most . . . understand intelligence to be *intellectual* in nature": Sternberg, R. "Prototypes of Competence and Incompetence." In R. Sternberg and J. Kolligian (eds.), *Competence Considered*. New Haven: Yale University Press, 1990.

p. 132

"'At nearly all-white . . .'": Woo, E. "California's Perilous Slide; Language, Culture: How Schools Cope. Home Life Plays a Crucial Role in Students' Success or Faiure." *Los Angeles Times*, May 18, 1998, p. R1.

p. 132

"'. . . we're not the ones who think that'": Dennis, B. "Cream of the Class of '99 Annual 'Celebration of Scholastic Excellence' Shows Top Achievers Graduating Northeast Ohio High Schools Also Know How to Party." *Plain Dealer*, Apr. 15, 1999, p. B2.

p. 132

". . . adolescence as a time . . ." Erikson, E. *Identity, Youth, and Crisis*. New York: Norton, 1986.

p. 133

"'Jocks (Athletes) . . .'": Levin, S. "A Hard Time for the Out Crowd." *Pittsburgh Post-Gazette*, May 2, 1999, p. A1.

p. 133

"'Why is it that we as geeks . . .'": *Pittsburgh Post-Gazette* (1999).

p. 134

". . . cliques exist . . .": Ekert, P. *Jocks and Burnouts: Social Categories and Identity in the High School*. New York: Teachers College Press, 1989.

p. 134
". . . one Texas community's . . .": Bissinger, H. G. *Friday Night Lights: A Town, a Team, and a Dream.*. New York: HarperCollins, 1999.

p. 134
"The message to students who value learning . . .": Fordham, S. *Blacked Out: Dilemmas of Race, Identity, and Success at Capital High.* Chicago: University of Chicago Press, 1996.

p. 135
". . . it is unlikely that teen culture will change . . .": O'Neill, B. "That's 'Mr. Geek' to You, Jock." *Pittsburgh Post-Gazette*, May 17, 1999, p. C1.

p. 136
"The gender stereotypes persist . . .": Sadker, M., and Sadker, D. *Failing at Fairness: How America's Schools Cheat Girls.* New York: Scribner, 1994.

p. 136
"'Math and science careers . . .'": Kunde, D. "From Geeky to Go-Go Girl: Changing the Perception of High Tech Careers." *Chicago Tribune*, Mar. 28, 1999, p. 3.

p. 137
"The perplexing problem . . .": Lobel, T., and Bempechat, J. "Children's Need for Approval and Achievement Motivation: An Interactional Approach." *European Journal of Personality*, 1992, 7, 37–46.

p. 137
". . . teachers call on boys . . .": *How Schools Shortchange Girls: The AAUW Report.* New York: Marlowe, 1995.

p. 139
". . . being accepted among their peers . . .": Selman, R., and Schultz, L. *Making a Friend in Youth: Developmental Theory and Pair Therapy.* Hawthorne, N.Y.: Aldine de Gruyter, 1998.

p. 141
". . . 'future time perspective'": Nuttin (1985).

p. 146
". . . adolescence is a time to test the limits . . .": Jessor, R., and Jessor, S. *Problem Behavior and Psychosocial Development: A Longitudinal Study of Youth.*" New York: Academic Press, 1977.

p. 146

". . . as these teenagers point out": Tucker, C. "In Their Own Words." *St. Petersburg Times,* June 23, 1999, p. D1.

p. 147

"'I explained to the Japanese teachers . . .'": Schupp, B. J., "Getting Schooled in Japan." *Baltimore Sun,* Nov. 11, 1998, p. C1.

## Chapter 8

p. 153

"You need to know . . .": Martin, J. *The Schoolhome: Rethinking Schools for Changing Families.* Cambridge, Mass.: Harvard University Press, 1992.

p. 154

"Expect your children . . .": Rosenthal, R. "Teacher Expectancy Effects: A Brief Update After 25 Years of the Pygmalion Experiment." *Journal of Research in Education,* 1991, *1,* 3–12.

p. 156

". . . stress the *processes* involved . . .": Nicholls (1989).

p. 159

"These excerpts . . .": "Next to Mom and Dad, It's a Hard Life (or Not)." *New York Times,* Nov. 7, 1999.

# Recommended Reading

American Association of University Women. *How Schools Shortchange Girls: The AAUW Report*. New York: Marlowe, 1995.

Arnold, K. *Lives of Promise: What Becomes of High School Valedictorians: A Fourteen-Year Study of Achievement and Life Choices*. San Francisco: Jossey-Bass, 1995.

Bruner, J., and Haste, H. (eds.). *Making Sense: The Child's Construction of the World*. London: Methuen, 1987.

Chen, C., and Stevenson, H. "Homework: A Cross-Cultural Comparison." *Child Development*, 1990, 60, 551–561.

Comer, J. *School Power: Implications of an Intervention Project*. New York: Free Press, 1980.

Fennema, E., and Sherman, J. *Fennema-Sherman Mathematics Attitudes Scales*. Madison: Wisconsin Center for Education Research, University of Wisconsin, 1986.

Fordham, S., and Ogbu, J. "Black Students' School Success: Coping with the Burden of Acting White." *Urban Review*, 1986, 18, 176–206.

Hill, P., Foster, G., and Gendler, T. *High Schools with Character*. Santa Monica: Rand, 1990.

Holloway, S. "Concepts of Ability and Effort in Japan and the United States." *Review of Educational Research*, 1988, 58, 327–345.

Lampert, M. "When the Problem Is Not the Question and the Solution Is Not the Answer: Mathematical Knowing and Teaching." *American Educational Research Journal*, 1990, 27, 29–63.

Lee, V., and Bryk, A. "Curriculum Tracking as Mediating the Social Distribution of High School Achievement." *Sociology of Education*, 1988, 61, 78–94.

Murphy, S. *The Cheers and the Tears*. San Francisco: Jossey-Bass, 1999.

Nicholls, J. "The Development of the Conceptions of Effort and Ability, Perception of Academic Attainment, and the Understanding That Difficult Tasks Require More Ability." *Child Development*, 1978, 49, 800–814.

Nicholls, J. "What Is Ability and Why Are We Mindful of It? A Developmental Perspective." In R. Sternberg and J. Kolligian (eds.), *Competence Considered*. New Haven: Yale University Press, 1990.

Nicholls, J., and Hazzard, S. *Education As Adventure: Lessons from Second Grade*. New York: Teachers College Press, 1993.

Peak, L. *Learning to Go to School in Japan*. Berkeley: University of California Press, 1991.

Rosenthal, R. "Teacher Expectancy Effects: A Brief Update After Twenty-Five Years of the Pygmalion Experiment." *Journal of Research in Education*, 1991, *1*, 3–12.

Rosenthal, R. "Interpersonal Expectancy Effects: A Thirty Year Perspective." *Current Directions in Psychological Science*, 1994, *3*, 176–179.

Rosenthal, R., and Jacobson, L. *Pygmalion in the Classroom*. Austin, Tex.: Holt, Rinehart and Winston, 1968.

Snow, C., and others. *Unfulfilled Expectations: Home and School Influences on Literacy*. Cambridge, Mass.: Harvard University Press, 1991.

Steinberg, L. *Beyond the Classroom: Why School Reform Has Failed and What Parents Need to Do*. New York: Simon & Schuster, 1996.

Stevenson, H. W., and Stigler, J. W. *The Learning Gap*. New York: Summit, 1992.

Stipek, D. *Motivation to Learn: From Theory to Practice*. Upper Saddle River, N.J.: Prentice Hall, 1988.

Vygotsky, L. *Mind in Society*. (M. Cole, V. John-Steiner, S. Scribner, and E. Souberman, eds.). Cambridge, Mass.: Harvard University Press, 1978.

Weiner, B. "Principles for a Theory of Student Motivation and Their Application Within an Attributional Framework." In R. Ames and C. Ames (eds.), *Research on Motivation in Education*. Vol. 1, *Student Motivation*. New York: Academic Press, 1985.

Weiner, B., Russell, D., and Lerman, D. "The Emotion-Cognition Process in Achievement-Related Contexts." *Journal of Personality and Social Psychology*, 1979, *37*, 1211–1220.

Werner, E., and Smith, R. *Vulnerable But Invincible: A Longitudinal Study of Resilient Children and Youth*. New York: Adams, Bannister, Cox, 1989.

# The Author

*Janine Bempechat,* an assistant professor at the Harvard Graduate School of Education, grew up in Montreal, Quebec, where she completed her undergraduate studies at McGill University. She received her master's degree and doctorate in education from the Harvard Graduate School of Education, where she has been teaching since 1986. She is interested in how parents influence their children to do their best in school. She has studied academic achievement and motivation in ethnically diverse groups of low-income children in both public and Catholic schools. A former National Academy of Education Spencer Fellow, her research has been supported by the National Science Foundation and the Spencer Foundation. She is a nationally noted commentator on educational reform, and she speaks regularly to parent and teacher groups around the nation.

# Index

Schooling, need to rethink, 11–12

Schoolwork. *See* Assignments; Homework

Science achievement: lag in, in United States, 1–2, 60, 65–66; sex stereotypes and, 135–138

Score@Kaplan, 95

Self-esteem: origins of concern with, 3–4; over-concern with, 2, 3–4, 65–66, 113; realities of, 113; through academic achievement, 3–4, 114–118; through extra-curricular activities, 9–10, 108–109, 112–118; underachievement and, 3–4

Sex stereotypes, 33–35, 135–138

Sex-segregated classes, 137–138

Shopping. *See* Grocery shopping and putting away

Singapore, 65

Single-parent families, 3, 109

Single-sex education, 137–138

Skiing, 48

Skill acquisition, encouraging, at home, 44–51

Smartness, children's beliefs about, 5, 19–33; effort and, 7, 24–28; helping with homework and, 78; onset of, 7, 24–25. *See also* Intelligence

Snow, C., 23

Social development, 153–154

Social problems in classroom, 97–98

Social promotion, 4, 114

Socioeconomic class, 64, 75–76, 99, 159–160

South Africa, 65

Sowell, S., 136

Spelling mistakes and instructional methods, 15–17, 85–86, 87–88, 104–105

Sports: athletic scholarships and, 126–127; involvement in, *versus* academic achievement, 114–118; valuing of, 7–8, 112, 134, 135. *See also* Extra-curricular activities

*Sputnik*, 61–62

Standards: college admissions, 10–11; high, as gift to children, 154–155; high, as indicator of high achievement, 137–138; high, teachers with, 89–93; low, origins of, 3–4; low, self-esteem movement and, 113–114; low, teachers with, 93–96; need to raise, 5; parent attitudes toward, 63–64. *See also* Expectations

Stereotypes: antiachievement ethic and, 132; labels and, 129–130, 133–134; race, class, and income, 64, 75–76, 132; sex, 33–35, 135–138

Stimulating experiences, 40–44, 50–51

Stories, sharing family, 130, 138–141, 157, 158–160

Stress: of college admissions standards, 119–126, 128; of extra-curricular activities, 108–109, 110–111, 161; lowered standards as response to, 113–114, 155; of rapid change, 151–152

Structure, for doing homework, 53, 54, 83

Struggle, gift of, 157–158. *See also* Confusion and frustration; Difficulty and challenge; Effort

Study groups, 149–150

Study skills, developing, through meeting difficulties, 53

Stupidity, children's beliefs about, 5, 6, 19–33. *See also* Intelligence

Suburban *versus* urban children, 64

Success: discussing pathways to, 130; sharing stories about, 130, 158–160; talking to children about, 28–33; talking to girls about, 33–35

Supplemental instruction: in cases of disagreement with teacher's methods, 88; in cases where teacher is too easy, 94–96

## T

Taft Union High, 132

Taiwanese students, academic achievement of, 1

Talking to children, 13–37; about effort and ability, 24–28; about failure to improve with effort, 35–37; about intelligence, 19–23; about mistakes, 14–18; about overcoming personal difficulties, 138–141; about success and failure, 28–33; guideline questions for, 166–167; influence of, 13–14, 151–164

Tantrums over homework, 82–84

*Teach Your Baby Math* (Doman), 41

Teachers: advocacy and, 98–103; assumptions of, questioning, 166; blaming of, 102–103; communication with, 103–106; disagreement with, handling, 85–106; disagreement with